Strangers

Essays on the Human and Nonhuman

" *Strangers* is an extraordinary, essential book. Both quiet and loud. Strange yet explicit. "

—Sara Baume

" These essays are sharp, purposeful, moving and strange: necessary writing for now. "

—Jenn Ashworth

" The writing in these essays is luminous and urgent, intensely intimate and wildly global. *Strangers* is an intricate exploration of environmental precarity, literary strangeness, and the importance of the nonhuman. "

—Naomi Booth

" *Strangers* is a work of generous, optimistic curiosity, one which forgoes the easy promise of a world to come and invites us instead into a relationship of charged "feral intimacy" with a world that is already here. "

—Sam Byers

" Rebecca Tamás has the ability to bring together our planet's environment with the ecology of the imagination, to retrieve silent life-forms alongside forgotten intellectual movements. "

—Amit Chaudhuri

Strangers
Essays on the Human and Nonhuman

Series edited by Robin Christian

Design and illustration by Patrick Fisher of Frontwards Design
Photograph by Robin Christian

ISBN 978-1-9160608-9-0

First published in 2020 by Makina Books, reprinted 2020
This expanded edition, first published 2022

'On Grief' previously published in *Somesuch Stories*
'On Watermelon' previously published in *Tribune Magazine*
'On Everest' previously published in *Extra Teeth*

Printed in the U.K by Henry Ling Limited, at the Dorset Press, Dorchester

Strangers:

"Essays on the Human and Nonhuman"

Rebecca Tamás

"Child be strange, dark, true, impure and dissonant. Cherish our flame."

Penda's Fen, David Rudkin

On Watermelon

7

On Hospitality

29

On Panpsychism

41

On Greenness

53

On Pain

65

On Grief

77

On Everest

93

On Mystery

105

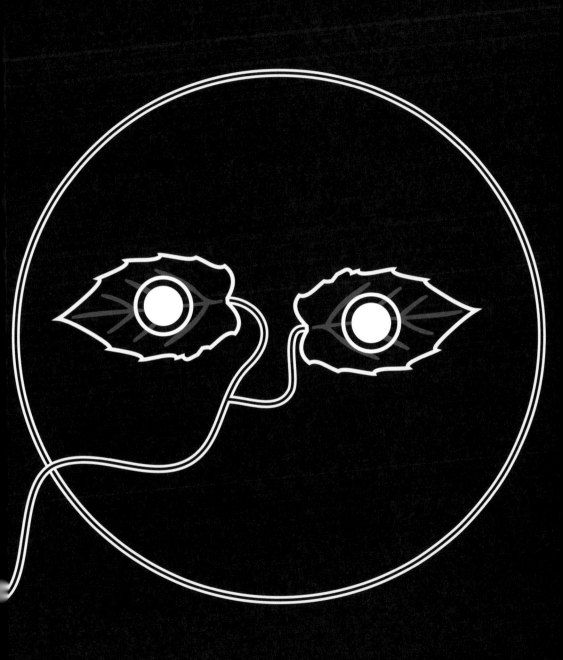

On
Watermelon

On Watermelon

When Adam delved and Eve span, who was then the gentleman?
—*Wat Tyler, leader of the Peasant's Revolt.*

At the beginning of April 1649, a political group calling themselves
the 'True Levellers,' (to differentiate themselves from 'The Levellers' an
alternative, somewhat less radical group) began a colony at St. George's
Hill near Cobham, Surrey. They began to till and sow the fields, with
"parsenipps, and carretts, and beans," [1] and to enact, in action, one of
their leader's central ideas in flesh – the earth as "a common treasury for
all, without respect of persons." They were nicknamed 'The Diggers,' and
have been known as such ever since.

The Diggers of 1649 began their cultivation of this common land seven
years after the start of the English Civil War and two months after the
beheading of the King, Charles I. It was a fractious, and revolutionary
time. Only two years before, in the Putney debates, commoners and
gentry discussed radical possibilities – suffrage for all, representation for
all. The country, brutally divided, was not only politically but religiously
split, seeing each side as working through God's plan for England; with
many wanting to create perfect righteousness on earth, so as to bring
forth the second coming.

As historian Daniel Johnson describes:

> The Diggers would thus till the commons and wastes of England
> collectively; withdrawing their labor from commercial society they

would decommodify social relations and establish the True Levellers' relationship with the earth. Once the common people saw the success of the Digger experiment, they would refuse to labor for wages any longer, and would work to create free associations of communist commonwealths in England and throughout the world. By "labouring in the Earth in rightousnesse together," the True Levellers intended to "lift up the Creation from that bondage of Civill Propriety, which it groans under." [2]

For the Diggers, the tumult of the period was an opportunity to create a form of Christian proto-communism: where wage labour, class hierarchy, economic inequality, the enclosure of common lands which threw peasants into destitution, private property, and landowner power, became things of the past. This would be achieved through shared cultivation, undoing the exploitation of the earth and humankind together. Winstanley explains these ideas, with others, in *The True Levellers Standard Advanced* of April, 1649:

> Break in pieces quickly the Band of particular Propriety [property], disown this oppressing Murder, Opression and Thievery of Buying and Selling of Land, owning of landlords and paying of Rents and give thy Free Consent to make the Earth a Common Treasury without grumbling ... that all may enjoy the benefit of their Creation ...

> ... Thy Mother, which is the Earth, that brought us all forth: That as a true Mother, loves all her children. Therefore do not hinder the Mother Earth from giving all her children suck, by thy Inclosing into particular hands, and holding up that cursed Bondage of Inclosure by thy Power ...

Propriety and single interest divides the people of a land and the whole world into parties and is the cause of all wars and bloodshed and contention everywhere ... [3]

The Diggers, through radical co-operation, wanted to build an alternative form of living, based on a community of human and nonhuman – a new vision of what a communal, earth centred radical society might look like, over 200 years before Marx and Engels published *The Communist Manifesto*.

The Diggers did not support female suffrage, yet they were, for the period, surprisingly radical in matters of gender equality, as well as those of class and rank. We see this in Winstanley's writing in *The Law of Freedom*:

> Every man and woman shall have the free liberty to marry whom they love...and neither birth nor portion shall hinder the match, for we are all of one blood, mankind; and for portion, the common store-houses are every man['s] and maid's portion.

> If any man lie with a maid and beget a child, he shall marry her. [4]

Yet, for all this prescient radicalism, the Diggers' tilling of the common land at St George's Hill lasted no more than four months. The Diggers were driven off the land by the military, local officials and landowners who were unhappy with their radical action. They then moved to Little Heath, but, confronted by many legal actions against them including indictments for riot, trespass, illegal assembly, and the illegal erection of cottages, the Little Heath Diggers gave up their settlement in the summer of 1650. Despite this brief span of activity, and the tumult of many other revolutionary groups at the time, they are still remembered. A Wigan 'Diggers Festival' runs every year, and they are held close by leftist groups still; Winstanley's name carved into Lenin's 1918 obelisk of 'great revolutionary thinkers.' The current of their thought continues through environmentalism and green politics; and is, if anything, more popular in such groups than ever before. Why?

For Winstanley, who was inspired to found the Diggers by 'divine' voices, England was in a truly fallen state. He looked back to the invasion of 1066 and the beginning of the 'Norman Yoke,' as the time when inequality became rife in the nation. As writer and academic Ed Simon explains:

> In Winstanley's understanding the commons were a feature of English rights, that had been violated in the development of privatization, whereby enclosures had begun to partition off formerly collective lands, which were now owned by individual aristocrats and noble families. The result, since the end of the fifteenth-century, had been increasing inequity, with the landless poor often not having space on which to graze their animals. There was an explicitly ecological gloss to Digger politics, with Winstanley claiming that "true freedom lies where a man receives his nourishment and preservation, and that is in the use of the earth." [5]

Winstanley was, however, not merely satisfied with the idea of returning England to a 'pre-Norman' state of equality. He sought to restore England to a 'pre-fall' level of godliness and purity. As he writes in a June 1649 letter to Commander Fairfax and his Council of War:

> The reformation that England now is to endeavour is not to remove the Norman yoke only and to bring us back to be governed by those laws that were before William the Conqueror came in … but … according to the Word of God, and this is the pure law of righteousness before the Fall. [6]

For Winstanley, this state could only be brought about when men and women were free to use the earth and its resources equally, not held in bondage by kings or landowners. He writes in *Fire in the Bush* in 1650:

> So long as the earth is intagled and appropriated into particular hands and kept there by the power of the sword … so long the creation lies under bondage. [7]

We know that the climate emergency is bad, we know that it is caused by carbon emissions, we know that biodiversity, nonhuman habitats, and human survival are all under grave threat. We also know that Western society is perpetually unequal and exploitative, and that, in the UK, the gap between rich and poor grows ever larger. But, of course, these two forms of awareness are actually the same thing. It is Western capitalism, the sequel to the Digger-era proto capitalism of land enclosure and wage inequality, that is the reason for every forest fire, every heatwave, every extinction. And this is why the Diggers continue to shadow our conversations about politics and environmentalism, the whispering echo of a world that could have been, that perhaps may be. What the Diggers make clear is that there aren't many competing issues that we need to absorb when we think about the rapacious cruelty of capitalist eco-crisis; the destruction of developing world ecosystems caused by Western emissions, the inability of governments to take real action, the rise of fascism, the ignorance of nonhuman reality, and nonhuman right to exist, the migration forced by rising temperatures and lack of water, the dearth of species. There is, to my mind, one issue that contains and expresses all of these concerns: *equality*.

Equality means the same opportunities of life and liberty for people of every race, nationality, sexuality, gender, physicality, age and place. It might also come to mean a radical equality that includes the nonhuman, the animals and beings, the trees and the rivers. The Diggers did not think of equality in this revolutionarily 'flat' way, but they did understand that exploitation of the earth, and exploitation of people, go hand in hand. A true equality would mean that Western countries pay for the homes of those living in India's flooding Sunderbans, or to support the families of Iranian farmers, killed by working outside in now regular 45 degree summer heatwaves, or offer reparations to the migrants of the Middle East, their grazing lands encroached upon by desertification. Activists know that human inequality and environmental inequality are one and the same. It is for this reason that in 2016, Black Lives Matter UK shut down London City Airport, when some of their members got on to the runway and chained themselves together. Black Lives Matter explained their protest, saying:

> Climate crisis is a racist crisis. 7/10 of the countries most affected by climate change are in sub-Saharan Africa. The UK is the biggest per-capita contributor to temperature change and among the least vulnerable to its affects. By 2050 there will be 200 million climate refugees.

The average salary of a London City airport user is €136,000 …
It is an airport designed for the wealthy. At the same time, 40% of
Newham's population struggle to survive on £20,000 or less. By
2020, there will be 200 million climate refugees globally. Whilst at
London City airport a small elite is able to fly, in 2016 alone 3,176
migrants are known to have died or gone missing in the Mediterranean, fleeing conditions that they did not create because cheaper,
easier and most importantly, safer avenues have been blocked by
the UK and other European countries. Black people are the first to
die, not the first to fly, in this racist climate crisis. Cut emissions.
Open borders. [8]

In 2019, the arguments of the 1600's, their battles over King or Parliament, seem like something from another planet. Yet, as they wrangled
over how to reach equality, so the activists of Black Lives Matter wrangle
over the same. In an apparently post-colonial, capitalist world, racism
is an issue of societal oppression *and* global destruction. The BLMUK
protest reminded us that the people of the developing world, long mar-
ginalised and exploited by Western powers because of race, imperialism
and prejudice, are experiencing environmental suffering due to the legacy
of this exploitation. We see this most sharply in Bolsanaro's destruction
of the Brazilian Amazon – where not only are the world's lungs being
destroyed by rapacious capitalism, but also the homes and lives of Brazil's indigenous Amazonian peoples. As the earth, the nonhuman world,
is polluted and destroyed, so too are the homes, livelihoods and communities of non-white peoples, who did nothing to bring this environmental
crisis about.

It is also crucial to remember that not only are non-white people's suffering *now* and into the future because of a climate collapse the West induced – they have been suffering from environmental exploitation for a long, long time. The theorist Kathryn Yussoff's book *A Billion Black Anthropocenes or None* interrogates the idea of an Anthropocene (a geological shift caused by human action) that begins with industrialisation. She argues that:

> The new modes of material accumulation and production in the Industrial Revolution are relational to and dependant on their *pre –* productive forms in slavery and its organization of human property as extractable energy properties … In this ledger of investment and the materialization of industrialization and empire sits an unseen, unrecorded history withdrawn from view in the syntax of slavery that foreshadows and reinscribes across all these relations of the globalization of capital. [9]

The spike in carbon emissions which 'begins' the Anthropocene, which we see at the start of the Industrial Revolution of Britain, and then other Western powers; did not actually begin when mills and factories and mines began churning out smoke. Rather it began when slave's bodies were forced into labour, their unseen work producing the riches which eventually made the process of industrialisation possible.

As Yusoff states:

> The Anthropocene might seem to offer a dystopic future that laments the end of the world, but imperialism and ongoing (settler)

colonialisms have been ending worlds for as long as they have been in existence. [10]

The inequality of climate collapse is part of the long history of inequality practiced by white, western peoples of means, against those without the resources to fight back. We see this in the 2016 protests against the Dakota Access Oil Pipeline in the US, which had the potential to pollute the Missouri River. The Native American Sioux people, and other indigenous peoples of Standing Rock, considered the pipeline a threat to the area's clean water and to ancient burial grounds. The native people, with support from allies and indigenous environmental groups protested the pipeline by putting their own bodies in-between the construction workers and the land; and building an indigenous camp at Standing Rock to create material and spiritual resistance against the pipeline, and to sue for Native sovereignty. They were met with attacks from police dogs, water cannons in freezing conditions, and brutal treatment from armed soldiers and police. Standing Rock's Historic Preservation Officer, LaDonna Brave Bull Allard, said of the protests:

> The U.S. government is wiping out our most important cultural and spiritual areas. And as it erases our footprint from the world, it erases us as a people. These sites must be protected, or our world will end, it is that simple. Our young people have a right to know who they are. They have a right to language, to culture, to tradition. The way they learn these things is through connection to our lands and our history.

> If we allow an oil company to dig through and destroy our histories, our ancestors, our hearts and souls as a people, is that not genocide? [11]

Tribal chairwoman Judith Bender argued:

> As a people that have lived in North America for thousands of years, we have environmental concerns about the land and drinking water … Our main concern is Iowa's aquifers might be significantly damaged. And it will only take one mistake and life in Iowa will change for the next thousands of years. We think that should be protected, because it is the water that gives Iowa the best way of life. [12]

Yet despite the persistence and efforts of the indigenous protestors, on 23 February 2017 the US National Guard evicted the entire protest camp. The pipeline was finished by April, and its first oil was delivered on 14 May 2017. The historical oppression of Native American people, their lack of resources, finances and political support, meant that despite their heroic efforts, they could not stop this potentially polluting pipeline being built in their sacred lands. Their human inequality, of race, imperialism and genocide, meant that their experience of their environment, and place, was also unequal.

Frantz Fanon wrote, when discussing imperialist oppression in *The Wretched of the Earth*:

> Wealth is not the fruit of labor but the result of organized protected robbery. [13]

The wealth of the oil company was, at Standing Rock, stolen from the indigenous people of the Sioux Nation.

As Winstanley reflected in *A Declaration from the Poor Oppressed People of England Directed to all that Call Themselves or are Called Lords of Manors*, in 1649:

> ... the Earth was made for us, as well as for you: And if the Common Land belongs to us who are the poor oppressed, surely the woods that grow upon the Commons belong to us likewise ... [14]

Equality lets indigenous American people have control over their water, and it lets indigenous dwellers in the Brazilian Amazon retain their homes, rather than giving over their forest to loggers. At the same time, this inequality keeps the fish in the rivers safe, draws carbon dioxide into the trees. When women across the world have access to birth control and abortion, to agency over their own bodies and determination over their lives, then the size of the population also falls, and the burden of humanity on natural life. True equality of this kind may be considered 'utopian,' but it is also material fact. What is good for human equality is good, overall, for nonhuman equality, for the survival of beings who cannot speak for themselves; but who are also living, and therefore have a right to live. This seems so obvious, and yet seems to need to be said.

Mark Fisher, in his book *Capitalist Realism: Is there No Alternative?* quotes a phrase attributed to Slavoj Zizek and Frederic Jameson: 'that it is easier to imagine the end of the world than it is to imagine the end of capitalism.' Yet, as Fisher argues:

> ... emancipatory politics must always destroy the appearance of a 'natural order', must reveal what is presented as necessary and

inevitable to be a mere contingency, just as it must make what was previously deemed to be impossible seem attainable. [15]

It is not that the suggestion of human and nonhuman equality is original or surprising, but rather that the possibility of its enaction seems, in daily life, impossible. We discuss technological carbon capture, 'hacking' the weather, increased nuclear power and alternative communities on other planets, as part of normal discourse. These far off, dangerous and/or wacky ideas get far more airtime in Western countries than any suggestion of genuine eco-socialism or radical environmental equality. Many agree that capitalism's inequality of resources and power is *quite literally incompatible with planetary survival*, and yet we do not seem able to begin to imagine its end.

The environmentalist and Sci Fi writer Ursula Le Guin famously said, in a 2014 speech at the National Book Awards:

> We live in capitalism, its power seems inescapable – but then, so did the divine right of kings. [16]

In 1649, the same year the Diggers set up their camp on St George's Hill, King Charles I was executed in Whitehall. Almost up until that very moment it seems that, for the people of England, and indeed for most of the people of Western Europe, the divine right of kings was the only form of power that was desirable, indeed *thinkable*. With Charles' death, suddenly, new and unfixed ways of being flooded into potentiality. The failure of Cromwell to be a good and just leader, and the restoration of the English monarchy in 1660, could not take away what had become possible for thought – which was a world without Kings. A world that came into being again, in 1789, in France.

The Diggers failed to create a new community of environmental equality in England, just as the peasants of the 1300's had failed to achieve freedom in the Peasant's Revolt. But they did change the parameters of what is thinkable, and in so doing have left behind potentialities we can access when we try and expand the thought that we are capable of.

Walter Benjamin, in his essay *Theses on the Philosophy of History*, writes that:

> To articulate what is past does not mean to recognize "how it really was." It means to take control of a memory, as it flashes in a moment of danger … The only writer of history with the gift of setting alight the sparks of hope in the past, is the one who is convinced of this: that not even the dead will be safe from the enemy, if he is victorious. And this enemy has not ceased to be victorious. [17]

Benjamin is right – we cannot know, 'how it really' was for the Diggers, whether, even if they had been somehow successful, their deeply Christian, and inevitably somewhat anthropocentric ideas, would have led to a world without rampant inequality, or racist oppression, or climate crisis. But we can also know that their past struggle, which we see echoed in the current struggles of those attempting to protect their lands and freedoms, will be destroyed by the present if we do not re-animate it.

Benjamin also writes, in the same essay:

> The tradition of the oppressed teaches us that the 'state of emergency' in which we live is not the exception but the rule. We must attain to a conception of history that is in keeping with this insight. [18]

We are in a state of climate emergency, environmental emergency, extinction emergency. Yet this 'state of emergency' did not arrive unbidden, or suddenly. This state of emergency has been existent throughout history – in the land enclosures that impoverished peasants, in the growth of Western economic power through the exploitation of the Atlantic slave trade, in the violence of colonial oppression, in the viciousness of global patriarchy and female silencing, in the abuse of natural resources by industrialist and post-industrialist landowners and businesses, in the cruelty meted out to the animals we eat – the crisis was always already occurring. The rising temperatures, natural disasters and bleached corals we see now, are only a new manifestation of the crisis of equality that is, as Benjamin says, 'the rule.' That does not mean that all of history has been the same, or that it can never change. Merely that our current crisis is not new, never could be new. The Anthropocene is a useful way to understand the start of the material change of the environment due to human action; but it only marks the visible appearance of systems of inequality that are much, much older.

My father was a dissident against Ceausescu's 'communist,' totalitarian regime in Romania, hounded by the secret police, spied on, and eventually exiled to Budapest. My Grandmother, once such a committed communist that she had gone to prison for it, had, by Ceausescu's time, lost all faith in the communist project as enacted by Russia and Eastern Europe. She had seen what they had done to her life, the life of her family, and of her nation. Yet, when Stalin died, on the 5 March 1953, my father remembers her weeping and wringing her hands. What was she crying for? A dictator who murdered millions? A man whose soldiers kept her native Hungary under their brutal control? I can't ask her now. But I think she was crying for what must have felt like, at the time, the death of a kind of thinking. The thinking that makes communal freedom, communal equality, communal joy, possible. In the perversion of Stalinism, the impossibly sharp hope of communism had seemingly been lost.

But such thinking, the thinking of equality, will always, zombie like, return from its frozen grave in the earth. It is for this reason that, in 1961, Frantz Fanon could write:

> What matters today, the issue which blocks the horizon, is the need for a redistribution of wealth. Humanity will have to address this question, no matter how devastating the consequences may be." [19]

The need for equality survives the critique of communism in practice, and it survives the naturalisation of a capitalist system driving the nonhuman world into the dust. The 'consequences' of redistributing wealth, of true equality, would be a very different world for the Western person than the consumer one they are used to. Whether that world would be one of no flying or cars, free public transport and allotments, or might have to be one of subsistence agriculture, no technology, no internet, no plastic and no money, I cannot say. It may depend how quickly we attend to equality for human people and nonhuman beings and landscapes; and whether we are able to speedily re-consider the value we place on living beings who are not us. We human beings love comfort, and such a radically different world may not be as comfortable as what we, in the West, currently experience. It might, however, be a world with many more forms of thinking available to us – of joy, of freedom, of pleasure, of community, of self-worth, and of love. Love for things that are nothing like us, and which may not love us back.

In 1650, after all the Digger settlements had been destroyed, Winstanley still felt able to write, in *A New Yeers Gift for the Parliament and the Army*:

> True religion and undefiled is this, To make restitution of the earth which hath been taken and held from the common people by the power of Conquests formerly and so set the oppressed free. [20]

The hope of equality was one which Winstanley enacted at St George's Hill, following his maxim in *A Watch-Word to the City of London and the Armie* that, 'action is the life of all, and if thou dost not act, thou dost nothing.' [21] But the destruction of his action did not wholly kill off his ability to hope, or his ability to see that a free, fair and non-exploitative relationship with the natural world, would be the strongest way to build a form of human freedom.

The conservative American journalist Warren T. Brookes, who came to prominence in the 1970's, is considered to have invented the term 'watermelon' as a pejorative name for eco-socialists, who are: 'green on the outside but red on the inside.' [22] Well, what could be better? Rather than separating them out into different factions and parts, this beautiful image gives us a vision of equality from all sides – human, nonhuman, and delicious. It is these 'watermelon' ideas, of protecting and interacting with the earth with care, through communal social systems, and without landlords or gentry, that makes the Diggers' ideas retain their power.

Watching a polar bear drown as the ice melts around it, missing the once familiar calls of the swallows, their numbers reduced by insect die off, hearing the cries of a polecat as it burns in a brush fire, we are most often encouraged to feel pity. There is certainly nothing wrong with feeling sympathy with what is different, with the suffering, or the destruction, of nonhuman beings or entities. But pity is not enough, when the rights of those living things to live are being destroyed. If we were able to imagine them as equal – their pain equal, their rights equal, their agency equal; what other visions of living might become possible for *us*? If we could protect their existence not because they are cute, or pretty, or sad, but because they are? If we could give up some of what we own, so that the nonhuman could survive?

St George's Hill in Surrey, once the home of the Diggers, is currently, in an almost too perfect metaphor for where we are now, a gated community with huge private tennis courts and golf courses. Houses there can go for as much as *fourteen and a half million pounds*. This closed community is one of the most exclusive residential areas in the UK, home to celebrities such as Tom Jones, Elton John, Cliff Richard and Ringo Starr. Under the earth of their mansions and swimming pools, their Porsches and Pilates studios, lie specks of the soil the Diggers walked upon, dormant, waiting.

Winstanley asked, in 1649's *The New Law of Righteousness*:

> Was the earth made to preserve a few covetous, proud men to live at ease, and for them to bag and barn up the treasures of the Earth

from others, that these may beg or starve in a fruitful land; or was it made to preserve all her children? [23]

There is only one true question, stirring and germinating underneath the ground of all the others, and that is it.

References

1   Letter from Henry Sanders, 16th of April 1649. Quoted in, p.44 *The Digger Movement in the Days of the Commonwealth*, Lewis H. Berens. Folk Customs Publishing.

2   Johnson, Daniel. *Winstanley's Ecology: The English Diggers Today*. p.14, Monthly Review - December 2013 (Volume 65, Number 7).

3   Winstanley, Gerrard, and Sandra Jones. The True Levellers Standard Advanced. Eugene OR: University of Oregon, 2002.

4   Winstanley, Gerrard, Thomas N. Corns, Ann Hughes, and David Loewenstein. *The Complete Works of Gerrard Winstanley*. Oxford: Oxford University Press, 2009.

5   Simon, Ed. "The English Diggers, the 'Commons,' and the Green New Deal." History News Network. Accessed April 2, 2020. https://historynewsnetwork.org/article/171387.

6   Quoted within: Camilla. "A Common Treasury for All: Gerrard Winstanley's Vision of Utopia." International Socialism, April 5, 2017. https://isj.org.uk/a-common-treasury-for-all/.

7   Winstanley, Gerrard, Thomas N. Corns, Ann Hughes, and David Loewenstein. *The Complete Works of Gerrard Winstanley*. Oxford: Oxford University Press, 2009.

8   Kelbert, Alexandra Wanjiku. "Climate Change Is a Racist Crisis: That's Why Black Lives Matter Closed an Airport | Alexandra Wanjiku Kelbert." The Guardian. Guardian News and Media, September 6, 2016. https://www.theguardian.com/commentisfree/2016/sep/06/climate-change-racist-crisis-london-city-airport-black-lives-matter.

9   Yusoff, Kathryn. *A Billion Black Anthropocenes or None*. Minneapolis, MN: University of Minnesota Press, 2018.

10 Yusoff, Kathryn. *A Billion Black Anthropocenes or None*. Minneapolis, MN: University of Minnesota Press, 2018.

11 Allard, LaDonna Brave Bull, and LaDonna Brave Bull Allard. "Why the Founder of Standing Rock Sioux Camp Can't Forget the Whitestone Massacre." Yes! Magazine, September 3, 2016. https://www.yesmagazine.org/democracy/2016/09/03/why-the-founder-of-standing-rock-sioux-camp-cant-forget-the-whitestone-massacre/.

12 Allard, LaDonna Brave Bull, and LaDonna Brave Bull Allard. "Why the Founder of Standing Rock Sioux Camp Can't Forget the Whitestone Massacre." Yes! Magazine, September 3, 2016. https://www.yesmagazine.org/democracy/2016/09/03/why-the-founder-of-standing-rock-sioux-camp-cant-forget-the-whitestone-massacre/.

13 Fanon, Frantz, Richard Philcox, Jean-Paul Sartre, and Homi K. Bhabha. *The Wretched of the Earth*. Cape Town: Kwela Books, 2017.

14 Winstanley, Gerrard, Thomas N. Corns, Ann Hughes, and David Loewenstein. *The Complete Works of Gerrard Winstanley*. Oxford: Oxford University Press, 2009.

15 Fisher, Mark. *Capitalist Realism: Is There No Alternative ?* Winchester, UK: Zero Books, 2010.

16 "Ursula K Le Guin's Speech at National Book Awards: 'Books Aren't Just Commodities'." The Guardian. Guardian News and Media, November 20, 2014. https://www.theguardian.com/books/2014/nov/20/ursula-k-le-guin-national-book-awards-speech.

17 Benjamin, Walter, Hannah Arendt, and Harry Zorn. *Illuminations*. London: The Bodley Head Ltd, 2015.

18 Benjamin, Walter, Hannah Arendt, and Harry Zorn. *Illuminations*. London: The Bodley Head Ltd, 2015.

19 Fanon, Frantz, Richard Philcox, Jean-Paul Sartre, and Homi K. Bhabha. *The Wretched of the Earth*. Cape Town: Kwela Books, 2017.

20 Winstanley, Gerrard, Thomas N. Corns, Ann Hughes, and David Loewenstein. *The Complete Works of Gerrard Winstanley*. Oxford: Oxford University Press, 2009.

21 Winstanley, Gerrard, Thomas N. Corns, Ann Hughes, and David Loewenstein. *The Complete Works of Gerrard Winstanley*. Oxford: Oxford University Press, 2009.

22 "Environment and Ecology." POLITICAL ECOLOGY. Accessed April 2, 2020. http://environment-ecology.com/political-ecology.html?start=8.

23 Winstanley, Gerrard, Thomas N. Corns, Ann Hughes, and David Loewenstein. *The Complete Works of Gerrard Winstanley*. Oxford: Oxford University Press, 2009.

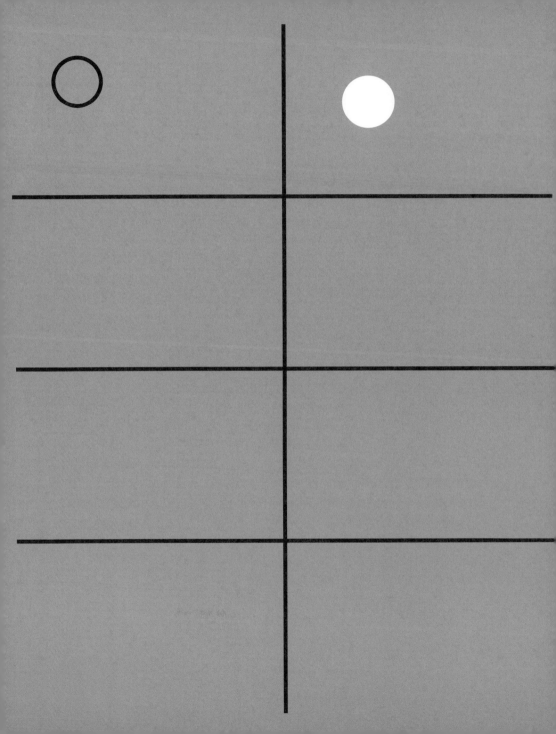

On Hospitality

On Hospitality

Never leave that country of rats and tarantulas and cockroaches, my
darling, where delight drops in thick drops of blood.
—Clarice Lispector, *The Passion According to G.H.* [24]

In Ancient Greece, hospitality – Philoxenia, or literally, 'friend to a
stranger,' was a central tenet of societal and religious life. The rituals of
hospitality meant that a Greek home should, when asked, take in any
weary traveller who might happen to be passing. The hosts were expected
to offer food, drink and a bath, and not to ask questions of the guest
until they had eaten. The guest was expected to offer respect, not make
burdensome demands, and to give a thank you gift, if they could afford
it. This practice was shadowed by the awareness that any guest could,
at any time, reveal themselves to be a god in disguise. The filthy beggar
slobbering into their soup could, in a moment, rip back their cloak to
reveal *Zeus Xenia* – meaning King of the gods, protector of travellers.

In Ovid's story of Baucis and Philemon, the couple welcome Zeus Xenia
and Hermes unaware; only realising they are hosting gods when they
notice that 'as often as the bowl was drained it was refilled of its own
will.' The hosts are 'astonished by the strangeness,' and terrified that they
may not pass muster. But their generous hospitality leads to monumental
reward – they are able to preside over a temple built on the spot where
their home is, and to die at the same moment, turned into trees which
will guard the temple entrance for eternity.

Such a system of hospitality contains a kernel of great risk: to let in someone potentially dangerous or disgusting into your home, even to risk displeasing a god. It is a system not built on pleasure, but on intimacy; an intimacy with strangers that rewards general survival and continuation and wellbeing, rather than individual fears. Might we meet the nonhuman with such hospitality?

For Timothy Morton, environmental philosopher:

> It isn't hard to love nature as an awe- inspiring open space. It's far harder to love the disturbing, disgusting beings who do not so easily wear a human face. Some of these beings are human. One task of the ecological thought is to figure out how to love the inhuman ... [25]

To adopt an ecological way of thinking – one that supports the full ecology of the planet, human and nonhuman – is to recognise the terrible intimacy of the nonhuman with us, and to accept this difference that rubs up against and inside us.

The Passion According to G.H., written by Brazilian author Clarice Lispector, tells the story of a young, dilettantish sculptor in Rio, known only by the 'G.H.' of her monogrammed luggage. Living a life of light-weight romances, parties and elegance, G.H.'s entire existence is interrupted and her entire being shifted. G.H.'s maid has left and, awaiting a new worker, she goes to the maid's room to clean it up. What she finds is an empty, scrubbed room, containing one brown and horrifying cockroach.

What happens to G.H. as she stares at the cockroach, which terrifies and disgusts her, is that the boundaries of her contained and individualistic selfhood begin to corrode. G.H. finds it almost impossible to communicate this experience, but she also feels she must use language to try and make sense of her new reality. For what G.H. has witnessed is that the mute, crawling life of the cockroach is deeply strange – the 'strange stranger' Morton describes but is also deeply intimate with her, indeed *is* her, and she it. The virulent life force within her and the cockroach is much more powerful than any flimsy sense of personhood she might have. Despite the intensity of her disgust, she does not turn away:

> I am the cockroach, I am my leg, I am my hair, I am the section of brightest light on the wall plaster—I am every Hellish piece of myself—life is so pervasive in me that if they divide me in pieces like a lizard, the pieces will keep on shaking and writhing. I am the silence etched on a wall, and the most ancient butterfly flutters in and looks at me: just the same as always …

> How opulent this silence is. It is the accumulation of centuries. It is the silence of the cockroach looking. The world looks at itself in me. Everything looks at everything, everything experiences the other; in this desert things know things. [26]

In this strange moment of nonhuman recognition, in the blindingly bright desert of true forms, G.H. finds the radical reality of intimate difference. She realises that part of her disgust at cockroaches, rats, flies, was the recognition of their mute life force which is mirrored in her own. G.H.'s hospitality to the reality of the cockroach— which she sits with and watches and makes space for— shocks and transforms her with the power of a revealed god. That transformation reveals the intimate strangeness of being which was always under the surface of her reality.

In terrified hospitality to the nonhuman, G.H. is able to experience truly 'ecological thought', the thought of a being who no longer anthropomorphises, who no longer orders the chain of being with humans at the top, who no longer longs to separate from the mass of beings which co-create her existence:

> We shall be inhuman - as humankind's greatest conquest. To be is to be beyond the human. To be a human being doesn't do it, to be human has been a constraint. The unknown awaits us, but I sense that that unknown is a totalization and will be the true humanization we long for. Am I speaking of death? No, of life. [27]

To have met something that was cute or beautiful, rather than disgusting, in the maid's bare room, would not have allowed G.H. to break into ecological thinking in this way. In the horror of the insect she sees the desperation of everything to *live*, the thread of being that knits throughout each creature and thing. It is this amoral potency which drives reality, not the structures of affection, elegance and society which she has so far lived by. G.H. rejects a false world in which we are kind to adorable puppies and sorrowful seal pups, but not crawling and stinging insects, and swarms of thrusting plants. This realisation, of unavoidable, constant intimacy with all that lives, is both agonising and fascinating for her:

> I'm blinder than before. I did see, I really did. I was terrified by the raw truth of a world whose greatest horror is that it is so alive that for me to admit that I am as alive as it is - and my most hideous

discovery is that I am as alive as it is - I shall have to raise my consciousness of life outside to so high a point that it would amount to
a crime against my personal life. [28]

What G.H. finds in 'horror' is the living reality of the moment. When she
first met the roach, she partially crushed it with the cupboard door, and
now, as she watches, white material squeezes, pus-like, from its body. In
the visceral disgust of this moment, G.H. witnesses the 'infernal' stuff of
the present moment, what is beyond the human, but also of it:

> What comes out of the roach's belly is not transcendable—ah, I
> don't want to say that it's the opposite of beauty, "opposite of
> beauty" doesn't even make sense—what comes out of the roach is:
> "today," blessed be the fruit of thy womb ...

> I want to find the redemption in today, in right now, in the reality
> that is being, and not in the promise, I want to find joy in this
> instant—I want the God in whatever comes out of the roach's
> belly—even if that, in my former human terms, means the worst,
> and, in human terms, the infernal. [29]

Thus what G.H. comes to is a form of consciousness deeply unfamiliar to
a Western mind-set (G.H.'s life in Rio is very much one of the bourgeois
Brazilian elite, rather than that of Brazil's indigenous peoples) but deeply
familiar to religions and spiritual traditions of the East. Indeed, it is especially close to the perspective and practice of Zen Buddhism. Tim Lott,
writing about the work of the Buddhist Alan Watts, gives us an insight
into the basic perspective of Zen:

Zen [believes] that all life and existence is based on a kind of dynamic emptiness (a view now supported by modern science, which sees phenomena at a subatomic level popping in and out of existence in a 'quantum froth'). In this view, there is no 'stuff', no difference between matter and energy. Look at anything closely enough — even a rock or a table — and you will see that it is an event, not a thing. Every 'thing' is, in truth, happening. This too, accords with modern scientific knowledge. Furthermore, there is not a 'multiplicity of events'. There is just one event, with multiple aspects, unfolding. We are not just separate egos locked in bags of skin. We come out of the world, not into it. We are each expressions of the world … [30]

G.H., slumped on the floor of the maid's room, next to a spewing insect, witnesses this 'unfolding;' the deeply ecological realisation that we are part of the same event as nonhuman animals, as soil, as rocks. She witnesses the void not as an empty zone of despair, but as a dynamic space where elements interplay, connect, dissipate and refigure. Such a space is terrifyingly amoral, beyond good and bad, primal in its focus on bringing more life into existence:

> In the world there exists no aesthetic plane, not even the aesthetic plane of goodness. [31]

The hospitality G.H. has provided leads not to comfort and friendship, but to a radical meeting of beings, a compassion that transcends like and dislike. G.H. finds her shared animal interior, and in this 'Hell' a kind of ancient, transforming bliss. She opens up a part of her home, unaware, to this creature, and the hospitality she provides creates a new form of being in the world; where all life is linked in its profane existing.

G.H. enters into an understanding of what Buddhist monk Thich Nhat Hanh described as 'interbeing.' [32] This form of existence does not totally annihilate the experience of self, but it destroys the idea of the self as an individual, independent monad. In this way of seeing, all beings/things are *relations*, existent only in their links to other beings, processes and forms. In her hospitality to what seems unmistakably and horrifyingly other, G.H. finds the reality of her own shared being:

> Finally, finally my husk had really broken, and I was, without limit … To the edge of what I wasn't, I was. What I am not, I am. Everything will be within me … my life doesn't have a merely human sense, it is much greater … The world interdepended with me – that was the confidence I had reached: the world interdepended with me … [33]

Within such a mind-set, valuing the needs or desires of human beings over nonhuman creatures seems ridiculous, deluded. This is not because they are one undifferentiated mass of sameness, but because their powerful differences are linked in an intimacy of being, existing only in relation to each other. We of course know this to be true scientifically – that the gut bacteria inside us, the rivers and forests, the crawling insects, the soil and the biosphere make human life possible and liveable. We know, factually, that human beings depend wholly on an interconnected web of human and nonhuman actors and things, yet at the same time live as if this is not the case.

What G.H. reaches in her experience with the cockroach is an understanding that human ideas of reason and progress are only casings around the unspeakable purposelessness of existence. This purposelessness isn't, however, bleak – it is the purposelessness of a great piece of music, or a glorious mountain vista – meaningful, but with a meaning that cannot be fixed or fully explained, and which is unexchangeable. Purposeless, but not pointless. Into this ambient purposelessness comes an understanding of our radical interdependence and intimacy with nonhuman forces; viscerally and urgently alive in a space of constant becoming. In her terrified, disgusted and joyful hospitality to the other, G.H. takes herself, and us, finally home.

References

24 Lispector, Clarice. *The Passion According to G.H.*. Translated by Ronald W Sousa. Minneapolis: Univ. of Minnesota Press, 2000.

25 Morton, Timothy. *Being Ecological*. Cambridge, MA: MIT Press, 2019.

26 Lispector, Clarice. *The Passion According to G.H.*. Translated by Ronald W Sousa. Minneapolis: Univ. of Minnesota Press, 2000.

27 Ibid.

28 Ibid.

29 Ibid.

30 Lott, Tim. "Alan Watts – the Western Buddhist Who Healed My Mind – Tim Lott: Aeon Essays." Aeon. Aeon, April 2, 2020. https://aeon.co/essays/alan-watts-the-western-buddhist-who-healed-my-mind.

31 Lispector, Clarice. *The Passion According to G.H.*. Translated by Ronald W Sousa. Minneapolis: Univ. of Minnesota Press, 2000.

32 "The Insight of Interbeing." Garrison Institute, August 2, 2018. https://www.garrisoninstitute.org/blog/insight-of-interbeing/.

33 Lispector, Clarice. *The Passion According to G.H.*. Translated by Ronald W Sousa. Minneapolis: Univ. of Minnesota Press, 2000.

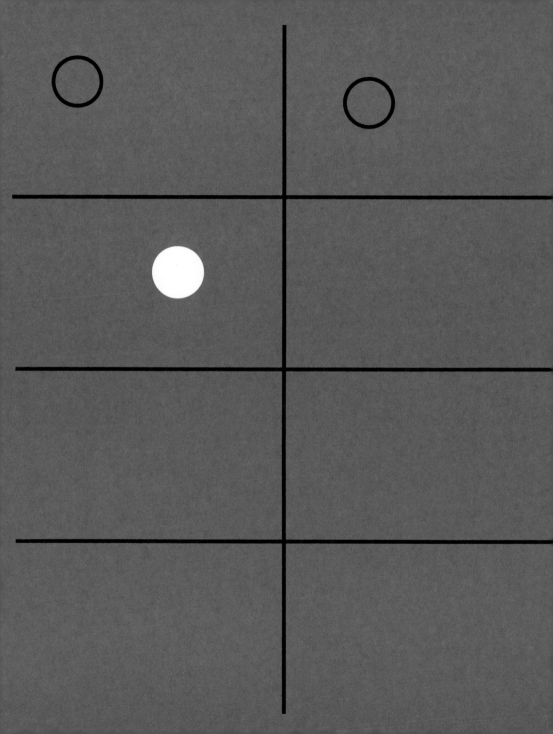

On
Panpsychism

On Panpsychism

When I go for a solstice swim on the south coast, I come out not feeling as refreshed as I might hope – still battling a summer cold, still worrying. Then, above our heads as we dry off, a skylark comes hovering – tiny against the rolling blue sky, hollering out its scratchy, buzzing, kaleidoscopic song. The grooves of my mind resettle, without being fixed – soda bubble brightness, wailing and rubbing song of liveliness and being alive. The bird has no interest in me, but his deliberate song is changing the font of my thought, taking my inwardness and flinging it open to the fizzing sea light. Nothing has changed, but, of course, it has.

The heavy movement and being of fog slows down my inner monologue, the spacious lushness of a forest in spring fills me with weird and pleasurable expansiveness, the cold shush of snow against the window clarifies me and empties me out. Can anyone really deny that thought and thinking comes from the outside as well as the inside? That when the outside is terribly damaged, the inside will be also?

Panpsychism is the theory that everything in nature has mind, or at least *mind-like qualities*. The arguments to support this range across philosophy and spirituality. Some animist religions see divine spirit in everything, some Christians see God's nature in everything he created – splinters of the great spirit in each part of the world.

For secular panscychists, a central argument is 'The Argument from Non-Emergence' described here by leading panscychist thinker David Skirbina:

It is inconceivable that mind should emerge from a world in which no mind existed; therefore mind always existed, even in the simplest of structures … "nothing in the cause that is not in the effect." [34]

Another closely related argument is that of 'Naturalised Mind:'

If the human mind is not to be considered an eternal mystery or a divine miracle, it must be fully, deeply and rationally integrated into the natural world. [35]

Do rocks think? Or do they at least have a will to, if not *life*, then being? The continuation of what they are?

Do trees, which communicate through roots and soil, which display 'crown shyness' (where they avoid touching each other's leaves in the high canopy) display a sensitivity to being, an ability to express their will, a goal-directedness, which we might consider sentient?

I don't know the definitive answer to these questions. But in the primordial mud which we came from, the chemicals, gases, atoms and electrons where we began, the potential for mind was there, impossible to locate or quantify. Waiting. We can't describe or rationally prove other minds in the mud, other 'desires' to live or to continue to be, but that doesn't mean that they aren't there.

*

When we think of the loss of ecosystems, of environments, of living beings, we most often consider the *practical* human cost. Or, if we are being generous, we consider this alongside the loss for the environment or creatures themselves, their suffering and destruction. But I want to add another consideration to these crucial ones, and it is the consideration of *mind*.

Sitting on the steps of my flat, crying. I feel awful – stressed, sad, but I don't know why. I can't locate a single pressing issue that has, over the last few days, suddenly pushed me into this low mood. The terror of blank misery rising up from nothing is worse than the emotions themselves. Slowly, slowly, sitting on the steps, I realise what is happening. These are not my emotions. Living closely, intensely, with my beloved housemate, I have *caught* her emotions. Fighting her internal difficulties as she is, not wanting to say outright what she is going through, or complain; her subconscious has nevertheless met mine. She does not have to tell me she is suffering for me to feel it in my body – wordless mind to wordless mind.

Is there not a version of this, infinitely more subtle and hard to parse, in the vibrations that we feel from the world beyond the human? We are not closed circuits, plastic wrapped – without words, things still speak to us, jolt us, pain us, free us, and change us. This isn't really surprising. The outside world, human and non-human, is not a painted backdrop to our lives and experiences, but makes them, is part of them.

*

David Skirbina, in *Panpsychism in the West*, quotes from a 1970 lecture by systems theorist Gregory Bateson:

[W]hen you separate mind from the structure in which it is imma-
nent, such as human relationship, the human society, or the ecosystem, you thereby embark ... on fundamental error, which in the end
will surely hurt you ... You decide that you want to get rid of the
by-products of human life and that Lake Erie will be a good place
to put them. You forget that the eco-mental system called Lake Erie
is a part of *your* wider eco-mental system – and that if Lake Erie
is driven insane, its insanity is incorporated in the larger system of
your thought and experience. [36]

The natural world is part of an intimate web of life that we share, but it
is also part of our mental web of existence, one that we ignore again and
again.

The unassailable difference of the nonhuman, is freedom from being
stuck in the unbearable feedback loop of the purely human, of our own
minds and selves, chatting away in a vacuum. When I was feeling deeply
ill in my mind and spirit, and I went and walked along a river in mid-
winter, was the movement of the water just a metaphor? Was it only a
distraction? I think that the river's cold flowing and rush was something
genuinely outside of the stultifying clamminess of my own head, and that
its cool *difference*, its ignorance of me, gave me relief.

We know that human health will suffer as we continue to expand cities
and reduce 'natural' or nonhuman environments and spaces. We know
pollution will choke us and make us sick. But what happens to thought?

The sheeny, various, prickling thought of fields of wildflowers.

The bellowing, vast, indelibly blue and subtle thought of storms out at sea.

The slicing, nervous, fruitful, bright thought of a primeval forest.

The layered, smooth, tingling, rich thought of humid wetlands.

The cold, to the point, attentive, virulent thought of a moor in winter.

Reading a novel in summer heat, looking out onto a deep Mediterranean blue bay, hornets and butterflies licking honey from the wooden terrace floor, changes my reading. The book hasn't changed, but my experience of it genuinely has. The cavities my thought is able to slide into, change.

What thought would have been impossible if Shakespeare had not had the memory of the slanting light of the forest of Arden, it's fuzzy, mud-thick equality of plants, animals and desires? What thought would not have been available to him, if Tagore had not travelled to the icy, sharply intense landscape of Himachal Pradesh's border with Kashmir, or the freeing blue horizon of rice paddies in Shantiniketan? What thought would have been buried without Virginia Woolf's time in the rolling hills of Sussex, clouds going in and out, bird noises, slash of water and the darting changes of the colours on the leaves?

With the death of different spaces, different environments, different histories and different bodily forms of moving through them, forms of thought die too.

We know that 'spending time in nature' is scientifically proven to improve human being's physical and mental health. Being in green spaces reduces depression, speeds up physical healing, and tackles anxiety.

Are such powerful impacts simply created only by the quiet of 'natural' places? The relaxation of pretty trees and flowers? What *makes* these things relaxing? After all, even *looking at pictures of nonhuman environments* has been proven to have beneficial impacts, balancing our parasympathetic nervous system.

Could it be then, that nonhuman difference itself is necessary to our mental wellbeing and the possibility of our thought? That we crave to not exist as lonely monads, but as individuals whose worldviews don't cram every orifice of available thinking? If you had to spend your entire life inside, moving from building to building but never being allowed the possibility of being in the open air, you'd go mad. But why? You'd have company, vitamin D supplements, food. The human is only a part, and perhaps without the agency and indifference of the nonhuman, the capacity for thought curdles and gets sick.

The Ecological philosopher Timothy Morton argues:

> ... what matters isn't exactly *what* you think, but *how* you think ... Being mentally healthy might mean knowing that *what you are thinking* and *how you are thinking* are intertwined ... And maybe mental health and ecological 'health' are interlinked. I believe that humans are traumatized by having severed their connections with nonhuman beings, connections that exist deep within their bodies ... [37]

Whether the nonhuman world has 'mind' or not, its capacities, change-ability, agency and being have an impact on *what*, and *how*, we are able to think. However many jungles and wetlands we destroy, the nonhuman will not 'go away,' because it exists in our very own guts and on our very own skin. But the harder it is to find and access, the more ill, damaged, maimed and suppressed it is, the fewer opportunities we will have to grow new and spacious kinds of thinking. This is not a question of morality (that the nonhuman is somehow 'good' or ethically instructive) but a question of difference – the truth that we are not all that exists, that there is a radical and shocking alterity bound up in every physical and mental possibility we have.

*

We don't always get to decide the thoughts that we have. After a terrible year taking care of a family member who is physically and mentally ill, I am swimming in the choppy waters of Galway Bay. The water smashes over my head, filling my mouth will salt, knocking me against the stones, twirling me through dark water. Coming out, I'm laughing and joking, proud of myself for getting into the cold sea in only a standard skimpy swimsuit, as others ploughed through in wetsuits and goggles. But the equation of body + water has released types of thinking I don't want to have, nudging them from my subconscious through the jolt of wave on skin. I can hear, really hear, as if it's right next to me, the sound of a child crying, screaming. Where is it coming from? There is nothing but black sky and white boiling water. Then I realise that the wailing is actually in my own head, is me, is coming from inside, was already doing so, and now has become available to me. I crouch in the shower, shaking, old and new traumas swirled and spat out by the rough water. The thought has been wrestled out of me, vomited up onto the platform of my mind.

*

Walking home at night, drunk and bad tempered, to find the yellow eyes of a fox on me, and a jolt of sharp stink throws me back into myself.

Waking up to unexpected frost, and the hurried, selfish thoughts I was having momentarily evaporating into frozen attending.

Being surrounded by low sea fog, a haar, as I stroll home over Edinburgh's meadows, knee height lake of gossamer water, normality peeled back and the city made strange, as strange as it is.

Our minds, the minds of the nonhuman, the intricate ever shifting patterns of thought, millions of endless webs, endless changes in the pressure, the expanse. A tree doesn't think like a snake, or a stone, or an amoeba, or like us. The word 'think' begins to crumble and fracture under the weight of itself, under all of these different beings. One mind is never going to be enough for me. Never should be enough.

References

34 Skrbina, David. *Panpsychism in the West*. Cambridge, MA: The MIT Press, 2017.

35 Ibid.

36 Ibid.

37 Morton, Timothy. *Being Ecological*. Cambridge, MA: MIT Press, 2019.

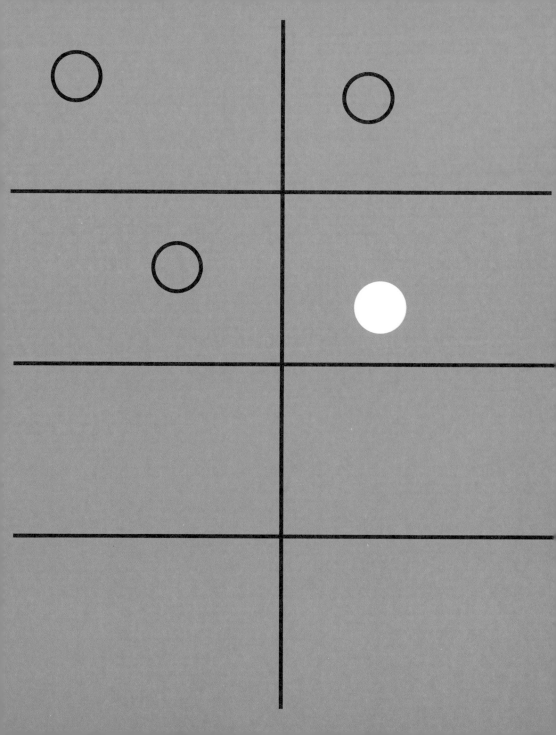

On Greenness

On Greenness

Face becoming green, leaves pouring out of its mouth, its eyes, berries dripping down, branches, whorls of foliage shaking the stone.

The 'green men' – foliate stone heads, sprouting plant life, are found in British churches and cathedrals, and in places of worship around the world, in India, Nepal, Borneo and beyond. The assumption historians of Christianity have made is that the British Green Man is an ancient pagan fertility figure who slipped into the worship of the early church, his reverberations continuing into the idea of Christ as the coming of life – the reborn shoot of god. As writer Mike Harding says:

> He is probably as old as mankind itself, always there, hidden in the woods, peering from the leaves. Puck, Jack in the Green, the Old man of the woods, or simply the Green Man: we know him without understanding him. [38]

But there are, were, many pagan fertility symbols, and the perpetuation and regeneration of this one tells us that the green man has power, feels necessary, important to hold on to even as the church tightened its grip over centuries.

Lifting my head up to the many green men teeming on the cloister's ceiling of Norwich's medieval Cathedral, it felt like the intimacy of the nonhuman was licking my skin – not the impossibly pure space of 'wilderness' or the controlled beauty of 'landscape,' but the human and nonhuman intertwined, bursting out of each other with discomfort, joy, pleasure. The human face becoming inhuman, showing the swirling movements beneath, where we become the other.

The Cuban-American artist Ana Mendieta broke these boundaries between the body and earth, between the human and nonhuman realms. Mendieta's 'earth art' involved the intervention of her body with live natural environments, the original artworks as fragile and perishable as that nature, often only recorded in films and photographs. In images from her *Silueta* series, which she called 'earth-body works,' the outline of her body is repeated and changed through different materials – water, foliage, shells, rocks, branches, earth, ice; red paint on cut out earth-works, bleeding into the dust, carved out of cracked ground, burning orange fire into the dark. In others, Mendieta's actual body is part of the art, she rises like a great pagan goddess of the soil in one of her *Tree of Life* pictures, entirely covered in mud, pressed against a huge tree trunk as if the lines between vegetation and body are fracturing and falling away. Or her body lies on the ground, every orifice sprouting white flowers, thickest where her genitals and face would be, sucked through and overrun by plant life, exploding outwards into the light. Or she slips beneath clear water, sunshine dancing on her limbs until the water and the figure become one. Or she comes towards us from a muddy, dark brown creek, covered in blood and feathers, face visible this time and staring with 'a wild surmise' fierce and knowing, in full control of her bodily agency, of her thrilling creative energies. Mendieta recreates herself as a Green Woman, in touch with the ancient or perpetual powers of the earth, blood and flame, sexual, brutal, tender and strong. Mendieta demonstrates Hildergard von Bingen's 'Viriditas,' the green force that is the kernel of life, that drives perpetual creation.

Mendieta's Cuban family fled the island when she was a teenager, and moved to Iowa in the USA, where she went on to study art. For Mendieta:

> Having been torn from my homeland during my adolescence, I am overwhelmed by the feeling of having been cast from the womb (nature)… My art is the way sI re-establish the bonds that unite me to the universe. [39]

Mendieta's earth art explored ritual and land, allowing her to reconnect, in places like Oaxaca, Mexico, to the spiritually diverse Latinx culture which she had been denied by her uprooting. This work was also a powerful rebuttal to the staid art world, making work that engaged with her position as a woman of colour in a white dominated culture, and drawing on the potency of her native cultures and perspectives.

Mendieta's work was also deeply feminist. She made strident, courageous art in response to a horrific campus rape at the University of Iowa, and she used her own body as a central tool in exploring violence against women. Indeed, it is depressingly necessary to note here that she herself would become a victim of the very oppression she interrogated; likely murdered by her husband, the sculptor Carl Andre, when she 'went out of the window,' after a fight in their New York home. He was acquitted, due to lack of evidence, but his terrible crime remains challenged by feminist groups throughout the world, asking 'Where is Ana Mendieta?' re-centering her art and her genius in a white and patriarchal art world which tried to suppress her memory.

Mendieta's concern with female selves and feminine suppression is, however, not only seen in the artworks that confront female abuse and destruction head on. These concerns also come to the surface in her 'green woman' creations. As she said:

> Through my earth/body sculptures, I become one with the earth ... I become an extension of nature and nature becomes an extension of my body. This obsessive act of reasserting my ties with the earth is really the reactivation of primeval beliefs ... [in] an omnipresent female force, the after image of being encompassing within the womb, is a manifestation of my thirst for being. [40]

Body pouring with leaves, lying naked in a Zapotec tomb in Oaxaca, or outlined in twisting black branches; this is the female form as spell – a magic able to unlock the powerful connection between human and nonhuman, not a passive carrier but an active force within the natural landscape. It is, even now, deeply enlivening and surprising to stare at these images, a woman coming from the earth, imperfect, unbounded, potent, totally in command of the flux of energy in which she moves.

She said:

> My art comes out of rage and displacement. Although the image may not be a very rageful image, I think all art comes out of sublimated rage. [41]

Even in the less 'overtly' furious earth art, there is the rage of loss, of being taken from your land, of having to exist as a woman of colour within a world of white supremacy. The earth art is not comforting and friendly but fierce and vibrating with power, body moving like lightning between forms, raging against containment, violence and suppression. A woman moving through the earth which is her right, a fury ripping through boundaries and rigidity, expanding into all the space which she might want to fill.

Mendieta does not use the natural elements of her artworks as mere 'fuel' for rageful creation however, it is always an interaction, a communication. She unlocks the feral intimacy of human and nonhuman that contemporary Western society so desperately tries to deny, allowing the green tongues to flail and wag. She said:

> I'm not interested in the formal qualities of my materials, but their emotional and sensual ones. [42]

Rage, sexual passion, love, drive the meeting of body and earth, where things are understood not with total rationality or logic, but with a potently curious emotional and physical response. The body is erotic in Mendieta's films and photographs, but so is the landscape. When we watch film of her lying in a creek in Oaxaca, it is not only her human form that seems sensual, but the water that flows over her like infinite hands, stroking her skin and the creek-bed at the same time; swarming and wanting, muddy with desire. Greenery explodes and emerges with both a devotional and an orgasmic energy, moving exciting, passionate; blurring the boundary between sexual expression and earthly eruption.

In the strange, anonymous Middle English poem *Gawain and the Green Knight*, a knight who is entirely green (not only clothes, but skin and body too) comes to challenge the noblemen of King Arthur's Court. He offers any of them the chance to strike a blow, and he will do the same afterwards. Gawain, probably thinking this will be an easy rout, overcomes the other's nervousness and cuts off the knight's head. The Green Knight promptly picks up his head, pops it back on his neck, and promises to meet Gawain in a year's time to do the same.

The significance of this supernatural knight's challenge, and the odd story of seduction and temptation that follows— where Gawain manages to avoid breaking his chastity in its entirety, and is rewarded with only a nick on the neck, rather than death— has been explained by literary scholars in uncountable ways; a Christian morality play, an exploration of the rules of chivalry. But what struck me, reading the poem for the first time as an undergraduate, is how Gawain is changed by his experience out in the greensward. Returning to the court, the king and nobles laugh at his journey, seeing it as a wonderful tale of bravery and success, but Gawain remains unsettled, distanced. He cannot forget what he has seen, the man made of plants, the rough, impossible to explain strangeness of what has happened, his own failings. The moral of the story is unclear and confusing, as if the very alienness of the experience is the heart of its meaning. The green figure will not give up its wisdom, or tell us how to interpret it.

The strangeness at the heart of Mendieta's work is similarly unbreakable. Her work flows through female expression, ritual, the power of the earth, the intimacy between human and nonhuman, the exploration of her native cultures, and much more, but it is never simply *about* one of these subjects. Like the Green Knight, she stares out at us from the foliage, a look of potent challenge on her face – asking us to come into a space that is not un-intellectual, but one that is suffused with irrationality; the sensuality of the body and the emotions, of the swirl and fracture of living beings of all kinds. We feel what she is asking of us, in her work, but cannot put it into words, the tug of the flame, of parts of ourselves which are not convenient or safe. The unruly, strange power of her work gives it a profundity that pretty landscape painting obviously lacks, the shiver of soil and bud, of being a stranger to yourself, of containing a strangeness you cannot name. Looking at Mendieta's work is seeing the huge realm of possibility that lies outside of the container of allegedly 'normal' existence in late capitalism – not a romantic idealisation of 'primitive' ways of life, but a space in which all can change, where the boundary between a wolf, a bird, a lizard, a woman is not as strict as one might imagine, but open and liable to shift. In Mendieta's work, as the philosopher's Deleuze and Guattari write in *A Thousand Plateau's*, 'The self is only a threshold, a door, a becoming between two multiplicities.'[43] Her art shows us that the 'natural world' does not wait outside of us, but moves through the door of our being, connecting and reforming what we are, its sticky difference impossible to excise. Her work is the promise of a green flourishing, another way of sharing with, becoming with, the world of which we are a part.

References

38 Harding, Mike. *A Little Book of the Green Man*. London: Aurum Press, 2006.

39 Institute of Modern Art Brisbane. "Ana Mendieta." Institute of Modern Art. Accessed April 2, 2020. https://ima.org.au/exhibitions/ana-mendieta-connecting-to-the-earth/.

40 Jones, Amelia. *Body Art - Performing the Subject*. Minneapolis (Minn.): University of Minnesota Press, 2007.

41 LaBarge, Emily. "Ana Mendieta, Emotional Artist." The Paris Review, March 13, 2019. https://www.theparisreview.org/blog/2019/03/08/ana-mendieta-emotional-artist/.

42 LaBarge, Emily. "Ana Mendieta, Emotional Artist." The Paris Review, March 13, 2019. https://www.theparisreview.org/blog/2019/03/08/ana-mendieta-emotional-artist/.

43 Deleuze, Gilles, and Felix Guattari. *A Thousand Plateaus: Rhizomes*. Berkeley, CA: Venus Pencils, 2009.

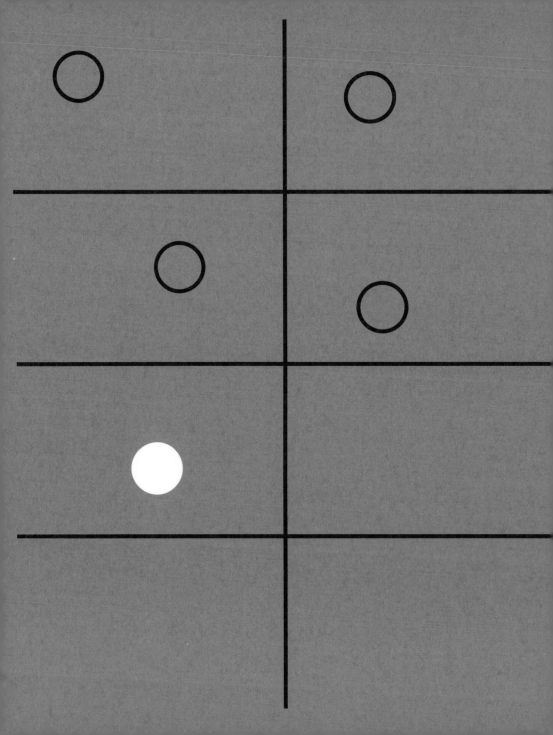

On
Pain

On Pain

I have to get to the other side of the animal.
—*Ariana Reines* [44]

In American writer Ariana Reines' collection of poetry *The Cow*, poetic language begins to assail the boundaries between human and animal, showing that the ways in which women are hurt connect up with the ways in which we treat animals in late capitalism. Reines' poetry, mixing prose and scattergun free verse; shows women's bodies and cows' bodies as viscerally exploited spaces, where the secret and terrible work of capitalist exploitation expresses itself in meat, blood and disease.

For the controlled and exploited women, and farmed cows, of the book, true bodily autonomy, true independence, does not exist:

> Cannot have a "the world" but can have millions of guts through which the maize and antibiotics of "a world" are forced to pass. [45]

The figures of this line produce the world of capitalism through the work of their suffering bodies, but they do not control it. Pain is the shared world which these bodies exist within.

To make clear the relationship between the ways in which female bodies and animal bodies are exploited, Reines contrasts, throughout the collection, a first person poetic voice of human experience, desire and trauma; with a third person voice of slaughterhouse manuals and veterinary instructions. Reines forces our faces into the way in which these women/animal bodies are understood as vehicles for pain, to entertain, pleasure or feed others than themselves. Bodies as forced spectacles or machines of pain:

> I asked him what he did ... He said, first I got some scissors and I cut part of her wig off. Then I tore off her wig. Then I punched her a few times in the skull. Then I threw her on the floor. She got up and I threw her on the floor again. When I hit her in the face finally she said something. She said, Oh my god, I think you've broken my nose. Then I got a screwdriver.

> ...

> One thinks of a cow living on grass ... but a cow does not, not so much, not in the United States. In the United States, after she has been alive about six months ... the cow lives on a feedlot, In Kansas for example ... She has got to shit where she eats, in the stall. In the stall she is fed FEED. FEED has many things in it, for example corn, lots of corn, and until recently, but maybe still, rendered animal. Rendered animal for extra protein. Also, antibiotics. The antibiotics make it possible for the cow to digest the corn, which, without antibiotics, would kill her, but which, with antibiotics, makes her fat, which is to say, TENDER. [46]

The woman abused by the man is treated 'like an animal' in that her body is merely a channel for him to pour his aggression into, human casing for the meat produced by her suffering – his pleasure.

The cow, a natural vegetarian, is forced to consume meat, surrounded by its own shit, its digestion made possible by being stuffed full of antibiotics. This queasy system is part of what caused foot and mouth disease in the UK, and is also part of the reason that antibiotic resistance is growing in human bodies. Even the corn the cow is fed, instead of grass, leads to dangerously singular crop reduction and high carbon emissions. The pain in the stomach and throat of the cow is the pain of the degraded human is the pain of the world choking on poison. Their unseen, or deliberately hidden pain is the engine powering our destruction.

Reines helps us to see that our unwillingness to confront female exploitation, oppression and sexual subjugation, is the same unwillingness that allows us to eat animals which come from farms nothing like those in storybooks – where animal bodies are not treated as living beings but as crude fuel.

> A cow is a name for a heavy woman or a woman with sloe eyes. Cow is a common epithet for a slow woman or clumsy woman; a woman with a foul smell. A thick-lipped woman, an unintelligent woman, a woman whose features possess a disturbing combination of ugliness and sensuality. A woman whose desire to fuck exceeds the desires of others to fuck her ...
>
> One who is ridiculous. Inherently ridiculous, irrespective of context. Or: What do you call the meat around a cunt. Often: a witness. Silent. [47]

A woman's body should betray only a facsimile of 'naturalness,' her makeup barely there, her skin glowing, her lashes long, her selfhood fixed and clean. She should not revel in, or express, her possible, flexible earth-bound natures – her hairy legs and pits, her damp vulva and its white-cream discharge, her hard soles, period blood, body odour and acne. She should not show anything close to virulent, untidy desire or pleasure, or enjoy food so much she gets fat, or be too open about childbirth and its piss and shit, or move or break genders, or add to or remove her breasts, genitals, hormones.

When she does allow these rebellious versions of herself to facome into the open, it is 'inherently ridiculous,' another opportunity to be silenced and closed down. To look at models in magazines and think of them as 'meat on the slab' has become cliché, familiar. But it is Reines' work that shows us what the real cost of body-as-meat is: the ways in which it shuts down agency, traps us into structures of punishment and disappearance. To bring this into the open means asking why almost every woman has either been raped, or knows a woman who has been; but why no men seem to know a rapist. The silence of the meat economy, of women on the slab, buzzing underneath the surface:

> Here is what happens when a cow is slaughtered. She has shit caked on her, she is led down a gently curved ramp, hundreds, thousands of cows are led down such ramps every day. If the slaughterhouse is a state-of-the-art facility … then the ramps will be curved in such a way that each animal can see two animals ahead, and not more, as they wait in line to be stunned, bled and processed. The knocker is first: The knocker administers a stun: a stun is a metal bolt shot into the brain … After the knocker knocks her, she is hung up by her hind legs and her throat is sliced open. She is bled on a moving conveyor belt. Everything happens very quickly. An animal is costly

... They cut the head off and slice the carcass in half. If there is shit on the outside of the animal, this is shit's chance to make contact with the inside of the animal. Therefore, disease. Disease is not the only derivative of her. [48]

The cow is knocked out, so as to miss the most intense pain of its own death; somehow smoothing away the guilt from all the other pain she has experienced, from her divided, miserable life in darkness, from her life-as-sickness. Reines writes, 'A wimple fell over the real as if to protect it.' [49] The real – these bodies in pain, compromised, used, slips into the back of our vision, the nonhuman feeding us quietly.

In the final section of Reines' book, the interplay between cow and woman, human and nonhuman, becomes less contrasting; and the bodies seem to merge into a fractured whole. It cannot be said to be a comforting or cheerful whole, rather it is a fiesta of pain, where comfort or relief comes only from expression – in the attempt to make the hidden known, and in the fight with language to make it express what it does not want to contain:

> An animal secretes a lot of cortisol if you harass he too much in killing
>
> her and this ruins the meat you are trying to turn her into
>
> If her flesh can be ruined by how marauded she feels can the air
>
> be ruined if she cries out inside it.

...

Who if I cried out

Who if I cried would hear me etc

...

What happens to an air that carries the screams of what is under

slaughter.

When she howls it's with her mouth.

When she howls it's with her mouth a tooth missing in it.

Menthol cigarettes and mozzarella cheese, coffee and sour apples.

Ma ma. MOUTH MOUTH.

...

Where

isn't she. Where isn't she inside her body. Where is she not. Where is

she least.

There was a whole body that went before me: It was her. [50]

The cries of the slaughterhouse merge with the cries of the poetic narrator, the animal/human boundary wavering and split, the suffering of exploited bodies under patriarchal capitalism made clear. The human was an animal all along, is animal, is infected by the virus of agony.

The body, put into a feedlot or suspended for sexual use and control, becomes truly *unnatural*, not in the sense of some vision of Eden lost, but in the loss of naturally occurring bodily freedom and independence. Misogyny feeds into animal cruelty feeds back into misogyny again – pain as a currency, because 'she likes it rough' or oppressive conditions are economically viable, fast, productive. The distance between real bodily experience, between reality and silence, gets ever bigger; narratives of fullness and delicious completion covering the systems which damage the earth and each body inside it.

The system of agriculture and meat production runs on a currency of pain and suffering, and we, quite literally, eat it up. Usually it is eaten by people that are hungry and can do no other. We go out, as women, into the world, swimming in our currency of pain; medical conditions misunderstood or ignored, sexual abuse or domestic violence hushed up, because we can do no other. But to bring it out into language, to see how the land, how the environment, how nonhuman beings and things suffer with us, for us, that is a kind of reach for freedom. It is a reach to understand what makes us sick, and to think about how we might get better, get well.

Reines finishes her book:

> I am harassed.
>
> …
>
> I am so tired, deep deep inside. I am tired.
>
> This ceaseless squabble. What Mandelstam said.
>
> What. Now what. go on. Go on. [51]

And we will.

References

44 Reines, Ariana. The Cow. Albany, NY: Fence Books, 2017.

45 Ibid

46 Ibid

47 Ibid

48 Ibid

49 Ibid

50 Ibid

51 Ibid

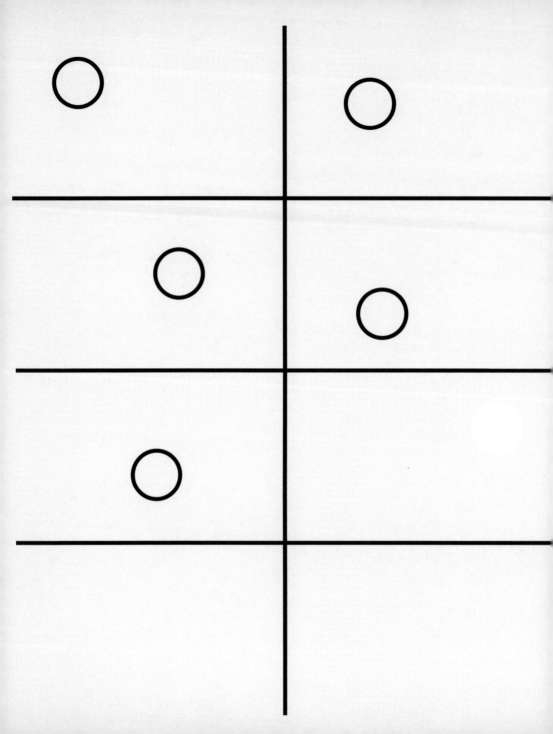

On
Grief

On Grief

Grief and depression are not the same. People who are not, or have not been, depressed, often seem to think of depression as a kind of sadness, a 'feeling blue.' But sadness is an appealing emotion to anyone with depression, because it denotes intensity, power of feeling, the possibility of being otherwise. Depression is not part of the happiness/sadness seesaw of human life. Better to call it by the name David Foster Wallace used, which is 'horror.' To feel truly depressed is to feel a creeping, miserable dread. No one who is profoundly depressed really believes that the tenor of their experience is 'just in their head,' whatever they may say to you. What they actually believe is that everything in the world is as profoundly squalid, vacuous and pointless as they feel, the terrible secret that the rest of humanity is covering up – that everything is a sham, that the world is *bad*.

In the film *Melancholia*, released in 2011 and directed by Lars Von Trier, a planet (also called Melancholia) is coming dangerously close to the earth, and this danger is impacting upon a dysfunctional American family. The central character of the film, Justine, played by Kirsten Dunst, is deeply depressed. At points she becomes catatonic, and is unable to enjoy her favourite foods, which turn to ash in her mouth. Her sister, Claire, is terrified that the planet Melancholia might hit the earth, but can also be comforted by her husband's assurances that it won't, moving between calmness and terror. Justine, however, does not seem terrified. She just 'knows' some things, including that the earth will be hit. Unlike Claire's swinging between grief, denial and panic, Justine is profoundly accepting of the earth's destruction. Indeed, she thinks that it is a good thing, as the earth is, in her words, 'evil.' At the end of the film, Justine is proved right, as the rogue planet crashes into the earth. As others cry and shake, she accepts it all, meditative and relatively at peace – the outside world finally matching the horror inside.

It is hard to describe the power of the impact this film had on me when I first saw it, in a cinema in Edinburgh in my early twenties. As the film ended I was convulsed with a hysterical sobbing, unable to move from my seat. The two friends who were with me had to sit holding my hands as ushers cleaned popcorn and wrappers from around our feet, for perhaps as long as fifteen minutes, when I was able to stand and take my crying to a toilet cubicle. The film was, quite simply, depression writ large on screen; the darkest parts of a depressed person's mind in bright colour and surround sound. To see that horror presented as a kind of sickly entertainment, made me nearly pass out. To be depressed, as I had been, but no longer was, is to see the world as horror – to know that we are cursed, that every good thing is a mirage, and every bad thing is the agonising truth, the pus filled wound under a clean dressing. All a depressed person really craves is for their Cassandra-like knowledge to be seen, understood by others. For the inherent evil of the planet and the people on it to flow out like corrupted blood. The film was a queasy celebration or vindication of this view, that the depressed were right all along, that destruction would be a purification of our falseness.

I was lucky. After having been a clinically depressed child, and teenager, at the age of 14 I began free, three times a week therapy, paid for by the NHS. I slowly managed to claw my way out of a depression that had not only had a hold of me, but which had defined my entire sense of self and experience of life. During that process, I remember my therapist asking me what I would like to get out of our work together. What I said was, 'all I would like is a neutral baseline'. I didn't want to be constantly jumping for joy; all I desired was to be sad when sad things happened, and to be happy when happy things happened – to base my feelings on my experiences of and interaction with the world, rather that feeling despair as soon as I woke up, before the day was even made.

Grief is the normal, healthy response of a person facing loss. The more intense the love was for the person or thing, the worse the grief is. Mourning is not a sickness, but a reaction to something terrible which has taken place. As my dear friend said, who recently lost her father, 'Grief is ok. Grief has to happen. It's everything else that it sets off, depression, anxiety, that is unbearable.' She would never want to not mourn for her father, but the pain of the loss is so intense that it can tip into periods of despair, to a depression that is not an outlet or a process, but a cycle of repetitive suffering and self-hatred. This is not to lessen the impact or intensity of what grief is, which is probably the most painful experience a human being can undergo; but to compare it to a despair which is not an expression and reckoning with loss, but a vortex of paralysing misery that leads nowhere.

An analysis by the *Breakthrough National Centre for Climate Restoration*, a think-tank in Melbourne, published this year, says that climate change is 'a near- to mid-term existential threat to human civilization,' and that there is a 'high likelihood of human civilisation coming to an end' [52] in 2050. No wonder then that more and more we hear the expression 'climate grief,' which writer Ellie Mae O'Hagan describes as:

... the sense that what climate change could bring is so massive, and so devastating, that people have begun to mourn; to slide into a state of abject despair. [53]

Yet, as we know from Freud, mourning and melancholia (depression/despair) are not the same thing, as O'Hagan's merged account of 'climate grief' might suggest that they are. As Freud writes in *Mourning and Melancholia*:

> ... when the work of mourning is completed the ego becomes free and uninhibited again ... The melancholic displays something ... which is lacking in mourning—an extraordinary diminution in his self regard, an impoverishment of his ego on a grand scale. In mourning it is the world which has become poor and empty; in melancholia it is the ego itself. The patient represents his ego to us as worthless, incapable of any achievement and morally despicable; he reproaches himself, vilifies himself and expects to be cast out and punished. He abases himself before everyone and commiserates with his own relatives for being connected with anyone so unworthy. He is not of the opinion that a change has taken place in him, but extends his self-criticism back over the past; he declares that he was never any better. [54]

At a certain point, a person who is mourning may be able to regain a sense of freedom and self-worth, even happiness; despite continuing to profoundly miss the person, place or thing they are mourning. The melancholic never reaches this point, turning against themselves, consumed with self-hatred and a sense that their entire life has been worthless. It seems to me, then, that a lot of what is called 'climate grief,' is actually a kind of climate despair or melancholia. Rather than mourning for what is lost, and being galvanized to try and protect what is left, we are, understandably thrown into a darkness that makes us revolt against our very sense of being in the world.

Neville Ellis and Ashlee Cunsolo are researchers into 'ecological grief.' They spoke to Inuit communities in the Inuit Land Claim Settlement Area of Nunatsiavut, Labrador, Canada. As they explain:

> [For the Inuit] the land is foundational to mental health. In recent years, melting sea ice prevented travel to significant cultural sites and engagement in traditional cultural activities, such as hunting and fishing. These disruptions to an Inuit sense of place was accompanied by strong emotional reactions, including grief, anger, sadness, frustration and despair.

One male who grew up hunting and trapping on the land in the community of Rigolet, Nunatsiavut explained:

> People are not who they are. They're not comfortable and can't do the same things. If something is taken away from you, you don't have it. If a way of life is taken away because of circumstances you have no control over, you lose control over your life. [55]

The Inuit of Labrador, their land and livelihoods fatally compromised by climate change, lose their sense of self – 'people are not who they are.' Their 'grief' over their land and culture has no end point, in the way that traditional grief might. They cannot, like they might with a beloved relative, think back on their happy times together, and mourn for the person's loss. They cannot enact the necessary rituals and goodbyes, then move on; leaving a space forever in their memory for the lost person, but regaining a sense of possible hope for the future. Because of the powerlessness of being victims of a crisis they did not create, grief slowly curdles into despair.

Ellis and Cunsolo also researched chronic drought conditions in the Western Australian Wheatbelt. They suggest that the farmers from the area experienced similar emotions to those of the Inuit of Labrador. They quote one of these farmers, who says:

> There's probably nothing worse than seeing your farm go in a dust storm. I reckon it's probably one of the worst feelings [...] I find that one of the most depressing things of the lot, seeing the farm blow away in a dust storm. That really gets up my nose, and a long way up too. If it's blowing dust I come inside - I just come inside here. I can't stand to watch it.
>
> Farmers just hate seeing their farm lift; it somehow says to them 'I'm a bad farmer'. And I think all farmers are good farmers. They all try their hardest to be. They all love their land. [56]

The Inuit and the Australian farmers are at the sharp end of ecological loss and destruction. For most Westerners, consumed by 'climate grief,' the impacts are not so concrete, or so totally destabilizing. For us, 'climate grief' is a kind of luxury, suffering without losing our means of survival, yet. But the spectrum of emotion, despair, fury, even self-hatred or disgust, are similar. These feelings may be more speculative and general than the specific and terrible pain of the Inuit hunters and

Australian farmers, but that does not mean that the pain is meaningless. Looking at the Amazon burning, and thinking of our society's paltry efforts to recycle, to fly less, to not waste food, the sense of hopelessness and pointlessness can become overwhelming. The grief we feel when we see that unique ecosystem and home burn soon curdles into a terror that freezes us, which feels fatal.

Yet, despite the understandable misery, it is dangerous to simply accept that the destruction of climate change is spiralling us into despair, despondency, frozen horror. If one of the most common symptoms of depression is not being able to get out of bed in the morning, seeing no point to being in the world, then climate depression is profoundly unlikely to lead to any action which might avert the very worst of ecological collapse. As the coral reefs die off, insects perish, deserts expand, glaciers melts and temperatures rise, it's all too easy to be a Justine, watching the impending destruction of the world with a grimace of pleasure; wholly acquiescent to the suffering we feel we deserve. Of course this kind of despair elides not only the suffering of *other humans*, but of the nonhuman beings and habitats who will be crushed. But lying back and taking it, giving up, is extremely tempting given the titanic difficulties that we face, and given the fact that it will be, as it always is, the most vulnerable humans and nonhumans who suffer and die in the face of environmental collapse. It is deeply, profoundly *depressing*, and it infects every part of our lives.

Reading a brilliant contemporary novel, following the lives and loves of a group of young millennials, I suddenly feel I have to put it aside. I am two thirds of the way through, and climate crisis has not been mentioned. How are these erudite and articulate figures not talking and thinking about this, every moment of the day? I never finish the book, depressed, disheartened by the insistence of this problem that dwarfs all others, but which I do not feel well placed to solve. It is so easy, and normal, to feel this way.

When I was coming out of the worst of my own depression, as a teenager, I had a surreal experience. Sitting in a chemistry lesson, I (seemingly literally) watched the colour drain back into the world around me. The underlying grey tinge which accompanied my entire vision gave way to bright colours, pouring from the edges of the room into centre— the muddy brown of the desk, the rich blue of the sky outside, the fizzy yellow of my classmate's school shirts, the deep green of the textbooks on the shelf. Feeling that this must be some kind of strange hallucination, albeit a good one, I didn't mention it to anyone. It was only years later that I discovered that severely depressed people have 'impaired contrast perception,' [57] which may make the world seem more grey to them. My depression genuinely pulled colour from my experience, and made everything seem flat. So too may 'climate depression,' leech our pleasure in a world that seems to be fading, silencing the energy or passion we might need to involve ourselves in activism or environmental work and advocacy; allowing us to ask less of our politicians and our leaders. Being demanding takes energy, recognising the peril you are in takes energy too, and strength, to not give up. Energy for the force that keeps our heads above water. Most of us in the West are not Inuit or Australian farmers, at the sharp edge of a climate crisis which is pulling apart everything we hold dear, not yet. It is not for them to gather the energy to resist, it is for us.

Having been depressed since early childhood, getting better meant starting again as a human being. I had to actively 'fall in love,' with my friends, moving from distanced affection to real adoration, and I had to work out a sense of self that was not predicated on numb survival. This was not a straightforward or easy process, and I had, and continue to have, occasional lapses back into mental health issues. But to awake to a rich green reality, suddenly alive with meaning and potency, was a kind of revelation. The fierceness of my desire to be alive in a living world shocked me, and still does.

Unfortunately, I was growing up in a time of growing awareness of climate collapse. No huge planet 'Melancholia' is swinging into view to destroy us, but the diagnosis of pain and destruction is the same. 'Climate grief,' as it is represented in contemporary culture, is actually climate despair – a misery which shuts down our ability to think critically and to have any version of hope. This kind of despair is wholly understandable, whether driving climate scientists to curl up in the foetal position as they read their own findings; or assailing environmental activists as they see the new airport runway they tried to prevent being opened; or filling Inuit hunters as they try to teach their wisdom to their grandchildren on ever receding ice. Such feelings of despair should not be suppressed or silenced. But climate *grief*, as a force for change, mourning and moving to new possibilities, has not yet fully emerged in the Western imagination.

Seeing my friend suffer as she mourns her father, I can see that grief is the price of love. It is the terrible pact we enter when we agree to love a thing, and in all the happiness that might follow, it is there, waiting for us. To grieve for the ecosystems, beings and people destroyed by climate change, is to give them the dignity, respect and love which they deserve.

It is right that extinctions are met with mourning, that space is made in our emotions for the enormity of the loss. Grief is, at its heart, about the *other*, the thing, person or place that is lost, not the griever themselves. I was never more selfish or self-centred than when I was depressed, and that was not my fault.

Acts of true climate grief are being seen, small shoots of direly needed mourning. In Iceland, this year, a group of around 100 people met to mourn and commemorate the melted Okjökull glacier. In the space where it once was, a plaque was erected saying:

> Ok is the first Icelandic glacier to lose its status as a glacier. In the next 200 years all our glaciers are expected to follow the same path. This monument is to acknowledge that we know what is happening and what needs to be done. Only you know if we did it. [58]

As people gathered to mourn the lost glacier, their mourning also gave birth to this memorial, which looks forward as well as back. This nonhuman wake was about deep and terrible loss, but also about what can be done, what must be done, to stop even more loss in the future— 'Only you know if we did it.' In this act of profound climate grief, Iceland showed the possibility for a genuine mourning that does not throw us into inescapable despair. This grief is the fuel to try and change the conditions in which we find ourselves. Grief may be the worst suffering a person can experience, and in its agony, we see the cost of doing nothing. If we have any wisdom we will try and heed the knowledge that such profound pain gives us.

I won't say we should find 'hope,' because that is a complicated thing when reasons for hope seem few. Also because forms of hope are different – some environmentalists hope for us to be able to carry on as we are, to crack some technological solution for carbon capture or mining or terraform which will allow rapacious capitalism to continue, as if climate change had never happened. The only thing they hope for is to return to their comfortable lives, without the fear of flood or fire. Their hope is for a 'sustainable' capitalism, a dream that can never truly come into being.

Some hope that, out of the miserable and disgusting mess that the West has made of the environment, might come more equitable, communal forms of society— not only reducing the harms of climate crisis, but creating better lives for human beings too, rooted in relation to the nonhuman world. Climate hope takes many forms, and none of the hopes seem likely.

Yet, when I think about the forms of society, politics, commons, equality, economy, education and environmental practices we would need to avert total climate collapse; I don't just think about the fact that we'd avoid widespread human and nonhuman death. I also think about the more joyful kinds of lives we'd be able to lead, if no-growth, equal societies sprung up around the world, protecting human and nonhuman alike, leaving the sky dark and wet with stars, letting the forest creep and the cities breathe. Because something is not likely, that doesn't render it impossible, or foolish.

Being numb will not help us, hating ourselves without action will not change things; despairing will (for those of us in the West) excuse our responsibilities to the global South, and the suffering they are experiencing because of the actions of our nations.

Grieving for the environment means, as Aldo Leopold explains in *A Sand County Almanac*, 'living in a world of wounds.' [59] It means rejecting total despair, but it also means giving up on any romanticised visions one might have had of an unblemished, pure natural world, where the human can turn to the nonhuman for relief and easy comfort. It means that, as Camille T. Dungy writes in *Black Nature*:

> ... there is no place in the land where one can idle inattentively or harbor romanticized views. Interactions with the natural world demand respectful, honest attention and vigilant care. [60]

The perspective Dungy describes is one of the black writer in nature, keenly aware of the land as beloved earth, *and* as a space of oppression and erasure. But a form of this critical, watchful, honest perspective is needed from every person, whatever their background—where there is no excuse to romanticise an environment perpetually wounded and in peril. In grief we feel the true pain depth of the wound, but still have room to try and heal it, if we can.

References

52 Gilding, Paul. "REPORTS." Breakthrough. Accessed April 3, 2020. https://www.
breakthroughonline.org.au/publications.

53 O'Hagan, Ellie Mae. "'Climate Grief' Is Real and I've Got It Bad." Vice, June 5, 2019.
https://www.vice.com/en_uk/article/gy48d4/environmental-grief-climate-change-anxiety.

54 Freud, Sigmund, and James Strachey. *The Standard Edition of the Complete Psychological
Works of Sigmund Freud*. London: The Hogarth Press and the Institute of Psycho-
analysis, 1957.

55 Ellis, Neville, and Ashlee Cunsolo. "Hope and Mourning in the Anthropocene:
Understanding Ecological Grief." The Conversation, February 27, 2020. http://
theconversation.com/hope-and-mourning-in-the-anthropocene-understanding-ecological-
grief-88630.

56 Ibid

57 Harvard Health Publishing. "The Quirky Brain: How Depression May Alter Visual
Perception." Harvard Health. Accessed April 3, 2020. https://www.health.harvard.edu/
newsletter_article/the-quirky-brain-how-depression-may-alter-visual-perception.

58 France-Presse, Agence. "Iceland Holds Funeral for First Glacier Lost to Climate Change."
The Guardian. Guardian News and Media, August 19, 2019. https://www.theguardian.
com/world/2019/aug/19/iceland-holds-funeral-for-first-glacier-lost-to-climate-change.

59 Leopold, Aldo Starker. *A Sand Country Almanac: and Sketches Here and There*. Oxford:
Oxford University Press, 1989.

60 Dungy, Camille T., ed. *Black Nature: Four Centuries of African American Nature Poetry*.
Athens: The University of Georgia Press, 2009.

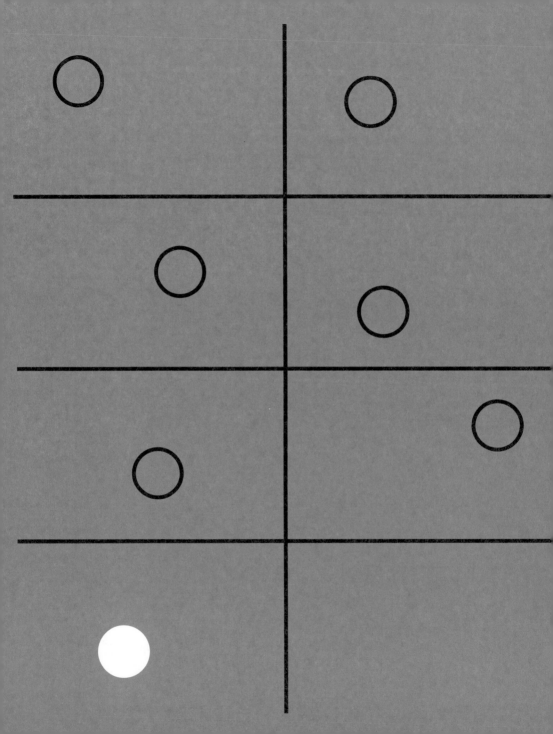

On Everest

On Everest

What men want to learn from nature is how to use it in order to wholly dominate it and other men. *Adorno and Horkheimer, The Dialectic of the Enlightenment* [61]

When we imagine it, the queues of climbers, the trash swirling around in the snow, the climbers stepping over or past dead bodies to get to the top, it is men that we imagine. White men, usually, because it is almost always white men climbing to glory. This is especially true now that many of Everest's current climbers are no longer experienced mountaineers, but rich people who have paid others to do almost all the hard work for them. Having no real interest in climbing any mountains but the one frozen, immense *celebrity* of nature, is the embarrassing big dick display to end all big dick displays. And people die from it.

Even for an experienced person, Everest is very hard to climb. It is this hardness that forms the appeal – whether for personal achievement, or for personal achievement and charity fundraising; it is the hardness that makes it impressive, and hardness which might encourage people to sponsor you, to make their donation 'worth it.' It might be just as hard to climb the stairs in a skyscraper thousands of times, and cost less, and be better for the environment, but that hardness is bland and unappealing. *I want to swing my dick at the top of the tallest mountain and know that I am real.* Such reality hunger has led to congestion to the summit, and to the necessity of a recent Nepalese clean up of the area, which collected 11 tonnes of rubbish and waste. 307 people have died on the mountain since 1922. In 2020, eleven people died in only nine days, trying to make it to the top. Corpses and trash have become part of the Everest 'experience.'

Not many people who *live* in and around a mountain see it as a spire on which to pin their ego. It might be hated, loved, feared, but it is part of a world. One of the first two people in the world to summit the mountain, the Sherpa Tenzing Norgay (who climbed with Edmund Hillary), described Everest as a 'mother hen.' [62] For him, the climbing of the mountain was, of course, an achievement, but he did not wrap his ego around the being of the mountain itself – describing it with the language of care, of tender knowledge.

Watching rich men risk their lives to climb, risk the happiness and security of their family and friends to do something that so many people have already done, is the ultimate spectacle of the Anthropocene. The mountain itself, its ecosystem, the local Nepalese community of Hindus and Tibetan Buddhists, the snow, the light, the air – these are not the point. The search for 'self actualisation' or triumph occurs on the most 'unreal' section of reality imaginable. Climbing to the top, jostling with others to get your tiny bit of space, your section where you can take a photo of yourself standing there mighty and alone, in shiny neon coloured jackets costing thousands of pounds. Mountaineering expert Maurice Isserman writes:

> There are more interesting mountains to climb. There are more beautiful mountains. There are more challenging mountains that are a better experience. But it's a trophy. It's the biggest. [63]

When asked why he was climbing Everest, the early British climber Edmund Mallory simply replied 'because it is there.' [64]

My friend Lily once said to me, 'if any bit of nature is Nazi, mountains are Nazi.' Of course, mountains themselves are not fascist, any more than trees are, but mountain's terror-inducing peaks have often been made to speak only of whiteness, of able bodiedness, of pure blood. The writer Richard Fuchs, writing in *Deutsche Welle* tells us:

> ... the German-Austrian Alpine Association, which was seen at the time as the voice of mountaineering, in the German Empire it was the first major sporting association to exclude Jews ... Flags bearing swastikas began flying over Alpine huts as early as 1924 - 10 years before Hitler seized power. The flags were followed by signs reading, "Jews not welcome here" ... Climbing expeditions, including the first attempt to reach the summit of Nanga Parbat in the Himalayas, were declared campaigns for Germany. Nazi propaganda pronounced that climbers would gain honor for Germany, or die trying. [65]

The cult of summits, of winning, of masculine valour, has never been very friendly to Jews, or to the queer, or to those of colour, or to those without perfect bodies or deep pockets. The Nazi propaganda of the Alpine Association had nothing to do with *actual* mountains, and everything to do with turning 'nature' into a vehicle for human dramas of triumph and purity of soul.

There are other very hard things to do rather than climb Everest. You could take a year out of your job and work with refugees coming in at Calais. You could take a year out of your job to work for Rape Crisis. You could work with Native American water protectors and other indigenous groups to try and protect natural resources from rapacious capitalist destruction. But somehow the executives and bankers and PR directors who climb Everest never do seem to take those options.

Everest is not for us, and that is why it is difficult to climb. We were never 'meant' to go there, are not designed to survive, do not belong. The vision of human endurance that we see up there is a pathetic expression of our inability to feel real in the reified world we have created, and of our desire to avoid the really hard things, which live inside.

An apocryphal story describes a man going to speak to a Christian hermit, who had spent the last 50 years in the desert standing on one leg, praying and suffering in subjection to god. The man asks 'how can you stay on one leg for that long? It must be so difficult!' The hermit replies, 'Oh no, this is easy. Loving your neighbour as you love yourself, now, that is difficult.'

Self-inflicted physical suffering is profundity and transformation as voyeuristic display. I want to scream 'get the fuck off of there!' Down here, in the messy realm of the human and nonhuman, is the unbearable challenge to love what is not us – each other, but also everything else; the beautiful mountains and the slimy worms, the shivering soil, the poisonous jellyfish. 'Nature' is not your achievement to be had, juddering ejaculation of parochial whiteness and self-congratulation.

My friend is a trained mountain guide, and when she came to my university for postgraduate study, she joined the climbing society. After the first trip, she was considering quitting. The young men of the group had insisted on climbing even though the conditions had turned, even though she had warned them it wasn't safe. As she went for her own long walk down below, enjoying streams, grasses and heather, they tried to climb the Scottish mountain and got horribly lost. They did not listen to her because she was a woman, and also because her attitude to the mountain was not one they recognised –

humble, interested, discreet. She put me in mind of Nan Shepard, careful watcher and walker of the Cairngorms who wrote in *The Living Mountain*:

> … often the mountain gives itself most completely when I have no destination, when I reach nowhere in particular, but have gone out merely to be with the mountain as one visits a friend with no intention but to be with him. [66]

Do the men who climb Everest want to fuck it? Is it the ultimate prize, that saves one from any fear of shame, of self-disgust? Who can say a man who has climbed Everest is not tough? Fucking the most beautiful woman alive will not be seen by almost anyone – but everyone gets to see this. It's the kind of thing they'd put in your obituary, the kind of thing your colleagues will chat about at the work Christmas party – 'Steve climbed Everest, and raised £5000 for dementia relief!' Raising money for charity is good. Dementia is bad. These things remain true, at the same time as climbing Everest becomes the most colossal missing of the point available.

I once did some trekking in the Andes, and it was beautiful, and tough. But what stays with me is sitting at base camp, at dusk, still surrounded by vegetation. Everyone else was busy cooking, and I sneaked away to sit with and watch the mountains. I learnt nothing, I have no profound spiritual wisdom to offer. I was a stranger too. But what I felt from the mountains was an intense, unutterably weird sense of presence. In my memory, I remember the mountains humming. Of course they probably weren't doing that – but my mind has a need to fill in something sensual to ground the intensity of that experience. The mountains were not looking at me, and I was nothing to them. I can't say what was there, but it didn't feel like a reflection of myself. It felt nothing like me, a language I couldn't parse, a being of which I had no access to, singing out over my head. Deep rumbling presence, the deepest base note imaginable, washed black and echoing. I did not get direct 'access' to the difference of the mountain's being, but observed that difference, circling outside of me, discrete, independent. Existent. Instead of climbing up, the able bodied, white display of moneyed mastery, could we not just sit down here for a second, and listen?

We cannot continue on with more corpses piles along the path to Everest, more rubbish for Nepalese citizens to clean up, more displays of flag waving, individualistic onanism. This attitude, of nature as a backdrop to our own triumphalism, is not only destroying this one mountain, but the world entirely. The plastic choking the coral reefs, the California wildfires, the floods in Bangladesh – the destruction of the environment is predicated on nature being perceived as something we *use*; whether that be to make ourselves feel special on a mountaintop, or something that gives us the raw materials for the objects we enjoy. It is exploitation, not cooperation or understanding. There is no mystery about what happens if we don't start to cooperate, listen, and work *with* nature – millions of nonhuman beings die, millions of humans die, and then, eventually, we all die. To watch people preen themselves on Everest is not only a spectacle, it is a warning. We have to manage the egoistic selfishness of capitalism, its desire to use up and spit out nature for its own ends, before it's too late. And it is those very people who climb Everest: the wealthy, the powerful, the strong, who hold these choices in their hands. It is up to them now to choose the stuff, the real stuff, of life.

References

61 Adorno, Max & Adorno, Theodore W. , *The Dialectic of the Enlightenment.* Stanford University Press, 2002

62 Tenzing Norgay. *Man of Everest.* G.P. Putnam's Sons; First Edition, 1955

63 Discovery Quotes Isserman on Everest Tragedy. Hamilton, April 25 2014. https://www.hamilton.edu/news/story/discovery-quotes-isserman-on-everest-tragedy

64 What Everest Climber Really Meant by 'Because It's There'. Adventure Journal, March 28 2017. https://www.adventure-journal.com/2017/03/what-everest-climber-really-meant-by-because-its-there/

65 Alpine club examines historical ties to Nazis. Deutsche Welle, 2 March 2012. https://www.dw.com/en/alpine-club-examines-historical-ties-to-nazis/a-16214770

66 Shepherd, Nan. *The Living Mountain.* Canongate Books, 2011

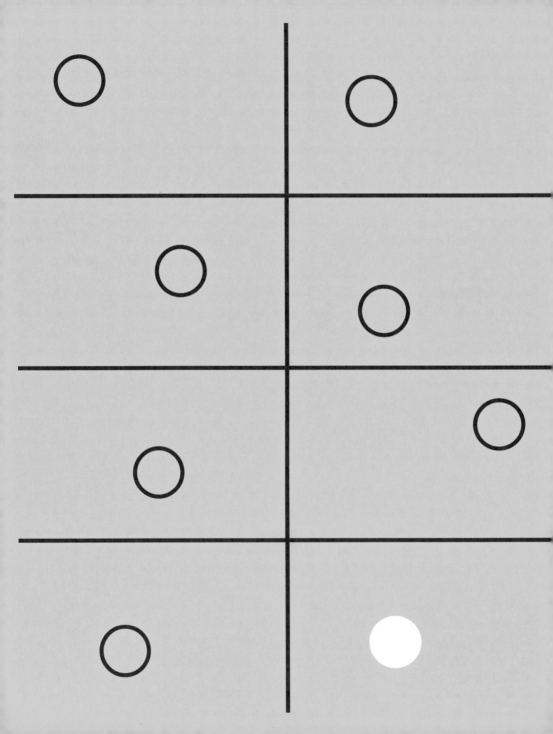

On
Mystery

On Mystery

I will always go to the funfair when it comes into town, and walk amongst the burger wrappers, and fizzy sweets, and Wurlitzers and clashing music. Occasionally a friend will agree to go on some rides with me and we'll scream until the air is glittered and swimming.

The feeling of entering a funfair is the feeling of utter inconsolable mystery. For a long time I have thought about what meaning I can ascribe to the hugeness of the feeling there; the sun going down as the rainbow coloured lights splash over the heath; the unsettling mixture of innocence and sex, where little children scream and play at the same time that teenagers gather to smoke and kiss and be sick. On the edges of the funfair are small dwellings, caravans and tents, white and blue washing hanging outside, leather boots. These are the normal, everyday things of the people who work for the funfair, but the funfair transforms them like a trick mirror; turning them strange, making them secrete mystery like phosphorescence.

Circus-feeling goes everywhere in which mystery dips into view. Seeing different stars every few days does not mean that you have always a good life. It cannot just solve your problems. Yet walking past a poster for one at the seaside, my partner says, 'we can't let you go to that, you'd run away.' He can see the vulgar, tender sparkling behind my eyelids.

At a circus in Budapest when I was very young, I saw lions and a real Indian elephant. I knew that I was being serviced with a brutality I couldn't get at home. I wondered whether Aztec citizens, watching sacrificial victims have their hearts cut out hundreds of years ago, felt any less terror or disgust than I might feel, if I saw the same thing.

Circus-feeling is saturated with meaning, but the meaning is unspeakable. I find myself wanting to write 'that feeling, that feeling, that feeling' over and over again as language pleasurably fails.

As a child I was terrified of ghosts. It didn't matter that there were real dangers out in the world, perverts, murderers, thieves. Every night I would lie choked in fear, listening for the smallest noise, knowing that this would be the moment when I would open my eyes and see one in front of me. The moment when I finally rid myself of terror was not the moment I stopped believing in them. Rather, it occurred to me to ask myself what they would do to me.

They might murder me, torture me, abduct me, maim me, make me go insane. Nothing they were capable of doing was any different to what a human might inflict, if they decided to do it. I had genuinely never thought beyond the moment of unspeakable terror and unknowing, where the veil would be rent and I would see … something. I did not actually know what. Imagining them cutting me into little pieces was awful, but without real mystery. If they wanted to kill me, I might not know the reason, but there would be one, somewhere. A plan, a rationale – cruelty, or sacrifice, or pleasure. Some sordid but nameable thing. So, I was free.

Mystery is in the tapes my father gave me of Transylvanian Roma music. The squall of the violins and the soaring voices is, in quite a literal sense, irresistible. I don't think you could walk in a forest, and see a huge snake rise up in front of you, and feel nothing. Similarly, I don't think you can hear this music and feel nothing. It is sophisticated, brilliantly put together, and wild. Where does the mystery come from? It is the music of no rulers.

When I first heard someone use 'gypsy' as an insult as a child, I was completely shocked. To me, to be a gypsy was the highest form imaginable for a human being – to keep moving, to parlay your own destiny out to the rattling of horses hooves, to head off to unknown places. A cosseted, privileged view of what is valued.

In W.G Sebald's *Austerlitz*, the title character remembers coming upon a ramshackle circus troupe, playing for a tiny audience behind the Gare d'Austerlitz:

> 'I still do not understand,' said Austerlitz, 'what was happening within me as I listened to this extraordinarily foreign nocturnal music conjured out of thin air, so to speak, by the circus performers with their slightly out of tune instruments, nor could I have said at the time whether my heart was contracting in pain or expanding with happiness for the first time in my life ... but today, looking back, it seems to me as if the mystery which touched me at the time was summed up in the image of the snow white goose standing motionless and steadfast among the musicians as long as they played ... beneath that shimmering firmament of painted stars until the last notes had died away, as if it knew its own future and the fate of its present companions' [67]

Walking through fields in Sussex, in high winds, trees moving, grass moving, air moving. White trainers getting black with mud, whistling, turbulent birdsong. My body clenched with the feeling that I am not the only one out there, something is moving through the green, not over it but … in it? Something is moving towards me and away from me at the same time, through the swirling blue patterns in the wheat, in the swirling patterns, around them. I recount this experience to a family member who I always consider to be rational, organised, sharp. Without looking up from cutting some bread she says, 'I suppose you felt Pan moving out there.' I immediately burst into tears. The softness and sentimentality of my reaction to this describes perfectly my biggest obstacle in talking to you. In really talking to you.

Pan has long been referred to as 'The God heard, but not seen.' This comes from the strange music he plays, pan pipes calling in the distance, underneath the sound of rainfall.

The Ancient Greek playwright Euripides wrote 'The Bacchae', a play which focuses on another wild god: Dionysus. In the play, King Pentheus of Thebes rejects the god and refuses to worship him; despite the fact that his power is demonstrated by the women of the city turning to the wild hills, to dance and sing in constant ecstatic worship of Dionysus. Pentheus ignores all warnings, bans the women's celebrations, and captures Dionysus, who being a god, easily escapes, and razes the palace to the ground. Deeply attracted by the Maenads who he claims to be repulsed by, and overcome by his enemy's casual destruction of all that he holds dear, he sneaks off to observe the women. Caught in an ecstatic altered state, his own mother, Agave, murders him, thinking he is a mountain lion. She is then sent into exile, whilst other family members are turned into snakes. By the end, even Dionysus' worshippers, the Bacchantes, feel bad for the harsh treatment meted out to those who refuse to give in to mystery. They want pity. But the play is not interested in pity, or mercy, or cruelty:

> Knowledge is not wisdom: cleverness is not, not without awareness of our death, not without recalling just how brief our flare is. He who overreaches will, in his overreaching, lose what he possesses, betray what he has now. That which is beyond us, which is greater than the human, the unattainably great, is for the mad, or for those who listen to the mad, and then believe them. [68]

Everywhere I go it seems like all the warnings and all the metaphors have already been written, and are waiting patiently for us to read them.

References

67 Sebald, W. G. *Austerlitz*. Edited by James Wood. Translated by Anthea Bell. London: Penguin Books, 2018.

68 Euripides. *The Bacchae of Euripides*. Translated by Charles K. Williams. New York: Farrar Straus Giroux, 19

Bibliography

Allard, LaDonna Brave Bull, and LaDonna Brave Bull Allard. "Why the Founder of Standing Rock Sioux Camp Can't Forget the Whitestone Massacre." Yes! Magazine, September 3, 2016. https://www.yesmagazine.org/democracy/2016/09/03/why-the-founder-of-standing-rock-sioux-camp-cant-forget-the-whitestone-massacre/.

Benjamin, Walter, Hannah Arendt, and Harry Zorn. *Illuminations. London: The Bodley Head Ltd, 2015.*

Camilla. "A Common Treasury for All: Gerrard Winstanley's Vision of Utopia." International Socialism, April 5, 2017. https://isj.org.uk/a-common-treasury-for-all/.

Deleuze, Gilles, and Felix Guattari. *A Thousand Plateaus: Rhizomes.* Berkeley, CA: Venus Pencils, 2009.

Dungy, Camille T., ed. *Black Nature: Four Centuries of African American Nature Poetry.* Athens: The University of Georgia Press, 2009.

Ellis, Neville, and Ashlee Cunsolo. "Hope and Mourning in the Anthropocene: Understanding Ecological Grief." The Conversation, February 27, 2020. http://theconversation.com/hope-and-mourning-in-the-anthropocene-understanding-ecological-grief-88630.

"Environment and Ecology." POLITICAL ECOLOGY. Accessed April 2, 2020. http://environment-ecology.com/political-ecology.html?start=8.

Euripides. *The Bacchae of Euripides.* Translated by Charles K. Williams. New York: Farrar Straus Giroux, 1990.

Fanon, Frantz, Richard Philcox, Jean-Paul Sartre, and Homi K. Bhabha. *The Wretched of the Earth.* Cape Town: Kwela Books, 2017.

Fisher, Mark. *Capitalist Realism: Is There No Alternative ?* Winchester, UK: Zero Books, 2010.

France-Presse, Agence. "Iceland Holds Funeral for First Glacier Lost to Climate Change." The Guardian. Guardian News and Media, August 19, 2019. https://www.theguardian.com/world/2019/aug/19/iceland-holds-funeral-for-first-glacier-lost-to-climate-change.

Freud, Sigmund, and James Strachey. *The Standard Edition of the Complete Psychological Works of Sigmund Freud*. London: The Hogarth Press and the Institute of Psycho-analysis, 1957.

Gilding, Paul. "REPORTS." Breakthrough. Accessed April 3, 2020. https://www.breakthroughonline.org.au/publications.

Harding, Mike. *A Little Book of the Green Man*. London: Aurum Press, 2006.

Harvard Health Publishing. "The Quirky Brain: How Depression May Alter Visual Perception." Harvard Health. Accessed April 3, 2020. https://www.health.harvard.edu/newsletter_article/the-quirky-brain-how-depression-may-alter-visual-perception.

Institute of Modern Art Brisbane. "Ana Mendieta." Institute of Modern Art. Accessed April 2, 2020. https://ima.org.au/exhibitions/ana-mendieta-connecting-to-the-earth/.

Jones, Amelia. *Body Art - Performing the Subject*. Minneapolis (Minn.): University of Minnesota Press, 2007.

Kelbert, Alexandra Wanjiku. "Climate Change Is a Racist Crisis: That's Why Black Lives Matter Closed an Airport | Alexandra Wanjiku Kelbert." The Guardian. Guardian News and Media, September 6, 2016. https://www.theguardian.com/commentisfree/2016/sep/06/climate-change-racist-crisis-london-city-airport-black-lives-matter.

LaBarge, Emily. "Ana Mendieta, Emotional Artist." The Paris Review, March 13, 2019. https://www.theparisreview.org/blog/2019/03/08/ana-mendieta-emotional-artist/.

Leopold, Aldo Starker. *A Sand Country Almanac: and Sketches Here and There*. Oxford: Oxford University Press, 1989.

Lispector, Clarice. *The Passion According to G.H.*. Translated by Ronald W Sousa. Minneapolis: Univ. of Minnesota Press, 2000.

Lott, Tim. "Alan Watts – the Western Buddhist Who Healed My Mind – Tim Lott: Aeon Essays." Aeon. Aeon, April 2, 2020. https://aeon.co/essays/alan-watts-the-western-buddhist-who-healed-my-mind.

Morton, Timothy. *Being Ecological*. Cambridge, MA: MIT Press, 2019.

O'Hagan, Ellie Mae. "'Climate Grief' Is Real and I've Got It Bad." Vice, June 5, 2019. https://www.vice.com/en_uk/article/gy48d4/environmental-grief-climate-change-anxiety.

Reines, Ariana. *The Cow*. Albany, NY: Fence Books, 2017.

Sebald, W. G. *Austerlitz*. Edited by James Wood. Translated by Anthea Bell. London: Penguin Books, 2018.

Simon, Ed. "The English Diggers, the 'Commons,'' and the Green New Deal." History News Network. Accessed April 2, 2020. https://historynewsnetwork.org/article/171387.

Skrbina, David. *Panpsychism in the West*. Cambridge, MA: The MIT Press, 2017.

"The Insight of Interbeing." Garrison Institute, August 2, 2018. https://www.garrisoninstitute.org/blog/insight-of-interbeing/.

"Ursula K Le Guin's Speech at National Book Awards: 'Books Aren't Just Commodities'." The Guardian. Guardian News and Media, November 20, 2014. https://www.theguardian.com/books/2014/nov/20/ursula-k-le-guin-national-book-awards-speech.

Winstanley, Gerrard, and Sandra Jones. *The True Levellers Standard Advanced*. Eugene OR: University of Oregon, 2002.

Winstanley, Gerrard, Thomas N. Corns, Ann Hughes, and David Loewenstein. *The Complete Works of Gerrard Winstanley*. Oxford: Oxford University Press, 2009.

Yusoff, Kathryn. *A Billion Black Anthropocenes or None*. Minneapolis, MN: University of Minnesota Press, 2018.

The author

Rebecca Tamás' poetry and criticism has been published in *The White Review*, *The Chicago Review*, *Some Such*, *The London Review of Books*, and *Granta*, amongst others. She is the editor, with Sarah Shin, of *Spells: Occult Poetry for the 21st Century*, published by Ignota Books. Her first full length collection of poetry, *WITCH*, came out from Penned in the Margins in 2019. It was a Poetry Book Society Spring Recommendation, a Guardian, Telegraph, Irish Times and White Review 'Book of the Year,' and a Paris Review Staff Pick. She is a former winner of the Manchester Poetry Prize, and the recipient of a Fenton Arts Trust Early Career Residency. Rebecca currently works as a Senior Lecturer in Creative Writing at York St John University, where she co-convenes The York Centre for Writing Poetry Series. She is represented by Emma Paterson, at Aitken Alexander Associates.

Acknowledgements

To Rachael Allen, for the many strange and beautiful conversations which fed into the writing of this book. To Tiffany Atkinson and Denise Riley for supporting my critical work as a doctoral student, where much of my ecological thinking began. To Emma Paterson, for her generosity, her belief in my work, and her kindness. To Katherine Angel, for her wise advice and thoughts on the early manuscript. To Sarah Shin, for shaping my knowledge of the universe.

To my family, for their unwavering support and love, especially my Mother, who inculcated my love of the natural world. To my friends, who keep me sharp and thoughtful.

To MH, who makes room for the weird.

Makina Books are an independent publisher currently based in London. Our publications, audio and audio-described projects seek to promote and celebrate independent and emerging voices—with a particular focus on poetry and nonfiction.

For more information on our forthcoming titles and projects please visit us at **makinabooks.com**